TABE® Strategy
Winning Multiple Choice Strategies for the Test for Adult Basic Education Exam

Copyright © 2018 Complete Test Preparation Inc. ALL RIGHTS RESERVED.

No part of this book may be reproduced or transferred in any form or by any means, graphic, electronic, or mechanical, including photocopying, recording, web distribution, taping, or by any information storage retrieval system, without the written permission of the author.

Notice: Complete Test Preparation Inc. makes every reasonable effort to obtain from reliable sources accurate, complete, and timely information about the tests covered in this book. Nevertheless, changes can be made in the tests or the administration of the tests at any time and Complete Test Preparation Inc. makes no representation or warranty, either expressed or implied as to the accuracy, timeliness, or completeness of the information contained in this book. Complete Test Preparation Inc. make no representations or warranties of any kind, express or implied, about the completeness, accuracy, reliability, suitability or availability with respect to the information contained in this document for any purpose. Any reliance you place on such information is therefore strictly at your own risk.

The author(s) shall not be liable for any loss incurred as a consequence of the use and application, directly or indirectly, of any information presented in this work. Sold with the understanding, the author is not engaged in rendering professional services or advice. If advice or expert assistance is required, the services of a competent professional should be sought.

The company, product and service names used in this publication are for identification purposes only. All trademarks and registered trademarks are the property of their respective owners. Complete Test Preparation Inc. is not affiliated with any educational institution.

Complete Test Preparation Inc. is not affiliated with the makers of the TABE ® exam, MCGRAW-HILL, INC®, which was not involved in the production of, and does not endorse, this product.

ISBN-13: 9781772450958

Version 6 Updated March 2020

Published by
Complete Test Preparation Inc.
Victoria BC Canada

Visit us on the web at https://www.test-preparation.ca
Printed in the USA

About Complete Test Preparation Inc.

The Complete Test Preparation Team has been publishing high quality study materials since 2005. Over two million students visit our websites every year, and thousands of students, teachers and parents all over the world (over 100 countries) have purchased our teaching materials, curriculum, study guides and practice tests.

Complete Test Preparation is committed to providing students with the best study materials and practice tests available on the market. Members of our team combine years of teaching experience, with experienced writers and editors, all with advanced degrees.

Feedback

We welcome your feedback. Email us at feedback@test-preparation.ca with your comments and suggestions. We carefully review all suggestions and often incorporate reader suggestions into upcoming versions. As a Print on Demand Publisher, we update our products frequently.

Find us on Facebook

www.facebook.com/CompleteTestPreparation

Contents

6   **Getting Started**
         The TABE® Exam   6
         A Better Score Is Possible   7
         Who does well on Multiple-Choice exams?   9

11   **Types of Multiple-Choice**
         Multiple-Choice Quick Tips   13

17   **Multiple-choice Step-by-Step**

19   **Multiple-choice Strategy Practice**
         Answer Key   38
         Reading Comprehension Practice   51
         Answer Key   65

74   **English Grammar Multiple-Choice**
         Verb Tense   74
         Common English Usage Mistakes   91
         Subject Verb Agreement   97
         English Grammar Practice Questions   105
         Answer Key   116

122   **Basic Math Multiple-Choice**
         Math Multiple-choice Strategy   123
         Practice Questions   128
         Answer Key   134
         Fraction Tips, Tricks and Shortcuts   140
         Decimal Tips, Tricks and Shortcuts   144
         Percent Tips, Tricks and Shortcuts   145

148   **Word Problem Multiple-choice Strategy**
         Types of Word problems   150
         Practice Questions   160
         Answer Key   163

167   **How to Prepare for a Test**
         Mental Preparation   169

172 How to Take a Test
    Reading the Instructions   172
    How to Take a Test - The Basics   173
    In the Test Room – What you MUST do!   177
    Common Test-Taking Mistakes   184

186 Conclusion

Getting Started with the TABE

CONGRATULATIONS! By deciding to take the Test of Adult Basic Education Exam (TABE®) you have taken the first step toward a great future! Of course, there is no point in taking this important examination unless you intend to do your best to earn the highest grade you possibly can. That means getting yourself organized and discovering the best approaches, methods and strategies to master the material. Yes, that will require real effort and dedication on your part, but if you are willing to focus your energy and devote the study time necessary, before you know it you will be finished the exam with a great mark!

We know that taking on a new endeavour can be a scary, and it is easy to feel unsure of where to begin. That's where we come in. This study guide is designed to help you improve your test-taking skills, show you a few tricks and increase both your competency and confidence.

The Test of Adult Basic Education Exam

The TABE® test comprises of three sections, Reading Comprehension, Mathematics and English. The questions are all in multiple-choice format.

The English portion has multiple choice questions covering sentence structure, spelling, English usage, punctuation and English grammar.

The math portion has multiple choice questions covering high school math areas, fractions, dividing, algebra, decimals, multiplying, probability, patterns, and basic geometry.

Test Strategy

This is a book about improving your score by using proven test strategies. This is different from other books such as a study guide, or a practice test. Even though we do provide lots of information to study and practice test questions, this book is about how to tackle multiple choice questions.

But do not worry - that is not all! While you are learning different strategies for answering multiple choice questions, you can also practice your skill at answering reading comprehension test questions English grammar and usage, and basic math, which are half your score on the TABE©.

Who Does Well On Multiple-Choice Exams?

With so many challenges working against you on the multiple-choice exam, what's the answer? Is there a way to improve your chances and your score? There is! The point of this book is not to discourage you, but to make you aware that there are strategies and tips that you can incorporate to raise your test score. Before we get into the specific strategies, let's take a general look at who does best on these types of tests.

>**Those who know the material.** This should go without saying, but the thing that will most raise your test score will be if you know the material that's going to be covered. While the strategies we'll discuss later will help you even with questions you're unsure of, the best thing you can do is learn the rules, dates, names, and concepts that you'll be tested on.
>
>**Those who have a calm, cool demeanor when taking a test.** Panicking can cause you to forget the information you think you know. Confidence goes a long way toward a better mark on multiple-choice.

Those who meditate or pray before the test. Don't laugh. It's a fact that people who meditate or pray, depending on their beliefs, enter a test room more confidently, and do better on the exam.

Those who operate on logic rather than instinct. Those who take a multiple-choice test based on instinct will be tempted to overlook the stated facts, and let emotion rule.

Those who have a system. Most of the book will deal with this, but you should not just guess randomly on questions you don't know. You must have a systematic strategy.

Types of Multiple-Choice Questions

EVEN IF YOU KNOW THAT A TEST WILL BE MULTIPLE-CHOICE, YOU STILL DON'T KNOW ALL THAT YOU NEED TO KNOW. There are various types of multiple-choice questions. Some tests will use just one of these kinds. Others will use several, or even all of them. Let's examine the various types of multiple-choice questions you are likely to encounter.

1. The "Who, What, Where Question." This is the simplest, most basic form of multiple-choice question. It asks for you to recall a single, simple fact about the material. For instance:

Where did the Wright Brothers fly their first airplane?

    a. Richmond, VA

    b. Kitty Hawk, NC

    c. Charlotte, NC

    d. Philadelphia, PA

The correct answer is B. This question simply asks for you to correctly identify a place name.

2. The "Multiple-Answer" Multiple-choice Question. This one varies from the "Who, What, Where" question in that more than one answer could be correct. It often appears like this:

Which of the following was not a declared war by the U.S. Congress?

I. World War I

II. World War II

III. The Korean War

IV. The Vietnam War

    a. I only

    b. I and II only

    c. III only

    d. IV only

    e. III and IV only

The correct answer here is E; neither the Korean nor Vietnam Wars were declared a war by Congress. These questions are tricky because many people are tempted, when they see a right answer, to select it, without thinking that there might be another answer that's also right.

3. The "Best Answer" Multiple-choice Question. On this type, the there might not be one clear objective answer, but rather, you're required to select the one that comes closest to being correct, or closest to what you believe is right. For example:

The factor which was the most to blame for the 1986 explosion of the Space Shuttle Challenger was:

    a. It launched too early in the morning.

    b. The cold weather allowed ice to develop.

    c. The astronauts did not have enough sleep.

    d. The astronauts were not adequately trained.

While it's entirely possible that C or D might have played a role, it's now commonly believed that the cause was the ice which had built up on the Shuttle's "O" rings. Some answers are possible, but B is the best answer.

4. **The "Fill in the Blank" Multiple-choice Question.** This is frequently used on grammar and reading comprehension tests. The question is presented as a sentence, with one or two key words left out. You must choose the correct one to fill the blank. Example:

The animals at the zoo _____ by the visitors.

    a. Did not feed
    b. Cannot fed
    c. Should not be fed
    d. Never feeding

The answer is C, since "The animals at the zoo should not be fed by the visitors" is the only one which makes good, grammatical sense.

Most the multiple-choice questions you'll encounter will fall into one above category, although it's possible you might also encounter a strange hybrid of two or three types. During your practice for the test, you should practice on each of these four types.

Multiple-Choice Quick Tips

Before looking at specific strategies in detail, lets first look at some general tips that you can use on any test and on multiple-choice questions in any subject. We will explore some of these in more detail later.

- **Finding Hints without Cheating** Pssst. There is a way to get hints about a question, even as you are taking the test—and it is completely legal. The key: Use the test itself to find clues about the answer. Here is how to do this. If you cannot answer a question, read the answers. If you find one that uses the language that your teacher or textbook used, there is a good chance that this is the right answer. That is because on complex topics, teachers and books tend to always use the same or similar language.

Another point: Look out for test questions which are like previous questions. Often, you will find the same information used in more than one question.

Occasionally you will find the answer to one question contained in another question - be on the lookout for this type of situation and use it to your advantage.

- **Before you try eliminating wrong answers, try to solve the problem.** If you know for sure that you have answered the question correctly, then obviously there is no need to eliminate wrong choices. If you cannot solve it, then see how many choices you can eliminate. Now try solving it again and see if one of the remaining answers comes close to your answer. Your chances of getting the answer right have now improved dramatically. Elimination is the most powerful strategy and we will discuss in more detail, as well as practice below.

- **Skip if you do not know.** If you simply do not know the answer and do not know how to get the answer, mark the question in the margin and come back if you have time.

- **Rule out answers that seem so general that they do not offer much information.** If an answer said, for example, "Columbus came to the West in the spring," it is probably not the right answer.

- **Use "all of the above" and "none of the above" to your advantage.** For "all of the above," you need not check to make sure all options are correct. Just check two of them. If two of the answers are correct, then this probably means they are all correct, and you can select "all." (This is not always the case, especially if there is also an option for "A and B" or "C and D."). Similarly, with "all of the above" questions, you only have to find one wrong answer, and then you have eliminated two choices - one is the wrong answer, and the other is All of the Above.

- **Let "close" answers be your guide.** The clever test-writer often includes an answer that is almost the correct one, to throw you off. The clever test-taker, however, can use this to his advantage. If you see two options that are strangely similar, then chances are good that one of these is the correct choice. That means you can rule out the other answers—and thus improve your chances. For instance, if two choices are George Washington and George Washington Carver, among Abraham Lincoln and Thomas Edison, there is a good chance that one of the two Washingtons is right. More on this strategy below.

Watch Out For Trick Questions

In general, most questions are what they appear to be and over-analyzing is a pitfall to be avoided. However, most multiple-choice tests contain one or two trick questions for a variety of reasons. A trick question is one where the test-writer intentionally makes you think that the answer is easier than it really is. Test-writers include trick questions because so many people think that they have mastered the techniques of taking a test that they need not study the material. In only a very few cases will a test have more than a handful of trick questions. Often instructors will include trick questions, where you really have to know your stuff inside-out to answer it correctly. This separates the "A" students from the "B+" students, and the "A" students from the "A+" students.

The best way to beat the trick question is to read the question carefully and break it down into parts. Then break it down into individual words. For instance, if a question asks,

> "When a plane crashes on the border between the United States and Canada, where are the survivors buried?"

if you had looked at each word individually, you would have realized that the last word, "survivors," means that the test writer is talking about burying people who are still alive.

Before You Change That Answer ...

You are probably familiar with the concept by now: your first instinct is usually right. This is why so many people, when giving advice about tests, tell you that unless you are convinced that your first instinct was wrong, do not take a chance. In those cases, more people change a right answer to the wrong one more often than they change a wrong answer to a right one.

How to Handle This.

Let's take that advice a step further, though. Maybe you do not always have to leave your first answer, especially if you think there might be a reasonable chance that your second choice was right. Before you go changing the answer, though, go on and do a few questions and clear your thoughts of the problem question. After you have done a few more, go back and start from the beginning. Then see if the original answer is still the one that jumps out at you. If so, leave it. If your second thought now jumps out at you, then go ahead and change it. If both are equal in your mind, then leave it with your first hunch.

Answering Multiple-Choice Step-by-Step

HERE IS A TEST QUESTION:
Which of the following is a helpful tip for taking a multiple-choice test?

   a. Answering "B" for all questions.
   b. Eliminate all answers that you know cannot be true.
   c. Eliminate all answers that seem like they might be true.
   d. Cheat off your neighbor.

If you answered B, you are correct. Even if you are not positive about the answer, try to eliminate as many choices as possible. Think of it this way: If every item on your test has four possible answers, and if you guess on one of those four answers, you have a one-in-four chance (25%) of getting it right. This means you should get one question right for every four that you guess.

However, if you can get rid of two answers, then your chances improve to one-in-two chances, or 50%. That means you will get a correct answer to every two that you guess.

So much for an obvious tip for improving your multiple-choice score. There are many other tips that you may or may not have considered, which will give your grade a boost. Remember, though, that none of these tips are infallible. In fact, many test-writers know these tips and deliberately write questions that will confound your system. Usually, however, you will do better on the test if you put these tips into practice.

By familiarizing yourself with these tips, you increase your chances and who knows; you might just get a lucky break and increase your score by a few points!

Answering Step-by-Step

It might seem complicated and unnecessary to follow a formula for answering a multiple-choice question. After you have practiced this formula for a while, though, it will come naturally and will not take any time at all. Try to follow these steps below on each question.

Step 1. Cover up the answers while you read the question. See the material in your mind's eye and try to envision what the correct answer is before you expose the answers on the answer sheet.

Step 2. Uncover the responses.

Step 3. Eliminate or Estimate. Cross out every choice that you know is ridiculous, absurd or clearly wrong. Then work with the answers that remain.

Step 4. Watch for distracters. A distracter is an answer that looks very similar to the correct answer, but is put there to trip you up. If you see two answers that are strikingly similar, the chances are good that one of them is correct. For instance, if you are asked the term for the distance around a square, and two of the responses are "periwinkle" and "perimeter," you can guess that one of these is probably correct, since the words look similar (both start with "peri-"). Guess one of these two and your chances of correcting selecting "perimeter" are 50/50. More on this below.

Step 5. Check! If you see the answer that you saw in your mind, put a light check-mark by it and then see if any of the other choices are better. If not, mark that response as your answer.

Step 6. If all else fails, guess. If you cannot envision the correct response in your head, or figure it out by reading the passage, and if you are left totally clueless as to what the answer should be, guess.

Watch out for this strategy if the test you are taking penalizes for wrong answers. Only a few tests do this, and if so, then guessing is NOT a recommended strategy!

There is a common myth that says choice "C" has a statistically greater chance of being correct. This may be true if your professor is making the test, however, most standardized tests today are generated by computer and the choices are randomized. We do not recommend choosing "C" as a strategy.

That is a quick introduction to multiple-choice to get us warmed up. Next we move onto the strategies and practice test questions section. Each multiple-choice strategy is explained, followed by practice questions using the strategy. Opposite this page is a bubble sheet for answering.

Answer Sheet

	A	B	C	D	E			A	B	C	D	E
1	○	○	○	○	○		26	○	○	○	○	○
2	○	○	○	○	○		27	○	○	○	○	○
3	○	○	○	○	○		28	○	○	○	○	○
4	○	○	○	○	○		29	○	○	○	○	○
5	○	○	○	○	○		30	○	○	○	○	○
6	○	○	○	○	○		31	○	○	○	○	○
7	○	○	○	○	○		32	○	○	○	○	○
8	○	○	○	○	○		33	○	○	○	○	○
9	○	○	○	○	○		34	○	○	○	○	○
10	○	○	○	○	○		35	○	○	○	○	○
11	○	○	○	○	○		36	○	○	○	○	○
12	○	○	○	○	○		37	○	○	○	○	○
13	○	○	○	○	○		38	○	○	○	○	○
14	○	○	○	○	○		39	○	○	○	○	○
15	○	○	○	○	○		40	○	○	○	○	○
16	○	○	○	○	○		41	○	○	○	○	○
17	○	○	○	○	○		42	○	○	○	○	○
18	○	○	○	○	○		43	○	○	○	○	○
19	○	○	○	○	○		44	○	○	○	○	○
20	○	○	○	○	○		45	○	○	○	○	○
21	○	○	○	○	○							
22	○	○	○	○	○							
23	○	○	○	○	○							
24	○	○	○	○	○							
25	○	○	○	○	○							

Multiple-Choice Strategy Practice Questions

THE FOLLOWING ARE DETAILED STRATEGIES FOR ANSWERING MULTIPLE-CHOICE QUESTIONS WITH PRACTICE QUESTIONS FOR EACH STRATEGY.

Answers appear following this section with a detailed explanation and discussion on each strategy and question, plus tips and analysis.

Strategy 1 - Locate Keywords

For every question, figure out exactly what the question is asking by locating key words that are in the question. Underline the keywords to clarify your thoughts and keep on track.

Directions: Read the passage below, and answer the questions using this strategy.

Free-range is a method of farming where domesticated animals roam freely, or relatively freely, rather than being kept in a pen or cage. Free-range can mean two different things depending on who you talk to. One definition, when talking to a farmer, is a technical description of a farming method. You may have seen free-range or free-run eggs in the supermarket. This is a consumer oriented definition. There are numerous benefits to farmers who practice free-range farming. Certification as a free-range producer allows farmers to charge higher prices and also reduce feed costs. That's not all - free-range methods also improve the general health of animals, which produces a higher-quality product. In addition, free-range farming allows multiple crops on the same land - another significant savings for farmers. Free-range certification is different from organic certification.

1. The free-range method of farming

   a. Uses a minimum amount of fencing to give animals more room.

   b. Can refer to two different things.

   c. Is always a very humane method.

   d. Only allows for one crop at a time.

2. Free-range farming is practiced

   a. To obtain free-range certification.

   b. To lower the cost of feeding animals.

   c. To produce higher quality product.

   d. All of the above.

3. Free-range farming:

   a. Can mean either farmer described or consumer described methods.

   b. Is becoming much more popular in many areas.

   c. Has many limits and causes prices to go down.

   d. Is only done to make the animals happier and healthier.

4. Free-range certification is most important to farmers because:

   a. Free-range livestock are less expensive to feed.

   b. The price of the product is higher.

   c. Both a and b

   d. The animals are kept in smaller enclosures, so more can be produced.

Strategy 2 - Watch Negatives

For every question, no matter what type, look for negatives. These can include never, not, and others that will completely change what is being asked.

Directions: Read the passage below, and answer the questions using this strategy.

Grizzly bears exhibit a common feature in nature, sexual dimorphism. This is where there are distinct difference in size or appearance between the sexes of an animal. Male grizzly bears, for example, generally weigh between 400 and 750 pounds, but can weight over 1,000 pounds. Females grizzlies are smaller, weighing 250 – 350 pounds, which is about 38% smaller. Female grizzlies stand about 3 feet at the shoulder, on all fours, and over 6 feet when standing upright. Males are bigger, generally standing 8 feet or more on their hind legs. Grizzlies in different geographical areas also show significant differences. For example, grizzlies from the Yukon River area in Northern Canada are 20% smaller.

5. Sexual dimorphism does not mean

    a. Male grizzly bears are the same size as the female of the species.

    b. All grizzly bears look the same and are the same size.

    c. Grizzly bears can be quite large, and weigh more than half a ton.

    d. All of the above

6. The size of a full-grown grizzly bear is never

    a. More than 500 pounds.

    b. Depends on the bear's sex.

    c. Determined simply by diet.

    d. Less than 8 feet tall.

7. Grizzly bears from the area of the Yukon River do not

    a. Get as big as most other grizzly bears do

    b. Get the rich and varied food supply needed

    c. Need the same nutrients as other grizzly bears

    d. Get less than 7 feet tall, and weigh close to half of a ton

Strategy 3 - Read the Stem Completely

For every question, no matter what type, read the information in the stem and then try to determine the correct answer before you look at the different answers.

Directions: Read the passage below, and answer the questions using this strategy.

Brown bears and grizzly bears are generally considered separate species, although technically, both are classified as Ursus Arctos. Brown bears live in coastal areas of North America where salmon is the primary food source. Bears found inland and in northern habitats are called 'grizzlies.' A sub species of Brown bears found on Kodiak Island, Alaska, have different shaped skulls due to the remote region and independent development.

Black bear, which are smaller and more common, are also a sub species, Ursus Americanus. Black bears are found throughout North America.

8. Grizzly bears, brown bears, and Kodiak bears are all

    a. Arctas Ursinas

    b. Ursus Arctos

    c. Arctos Ursina

    d. Ursula Arctic

9. Kodiak brown bears are classified as a different subspecies because

   a. They are much larger than other brown bears

   b. Their diet is radically different from that of other brown bears

   c. They are not true brown bears but instead a mixture of bear species

   d. Of their genetics and head shape, as well as their physical isolation

10. The term grizzlies, when referring to the brown bear, is used mainly

   a. In eastern areas where the bear grows large

   b. Only in snowy areas where there are low year round temperatures

   c. In the northern and inland areas

   d. In areas where the bear has a silver appearance

11. The term brown bear is normally used

   a. When one of the main food sources is salmon

   b. When the bear is small

   c. When the bear is found inland

   d. When the bear has a light brown coat and is very large

Strategy 4 - Consider all the Choices Before Deciding

For every question, no matter what type, make sure to read every option before making your choice.

Directions: Read the passage below, and answer the questions using this strategy.

Polar bears and grizzlies are different species although there are rare cases of hybrids. Scientists have known the two species are compatible for some time and there are several cases of hybrids in zoos.

In 2006, in Canada's Northwest Territories, a hunter shot what he thought was a polar bear. This bear, however, was slightly different. Like most polar bears, its fur was thick and white, as one would expect of a polar bear. However the bear also had some characteristics of grizzlies, such as long claws, a humped back, and brown patches around its nose, eyes and back.

This odd combination of features from both species soon attracted attention of the Wildlife Genetics International in British Columbia, Canada, which confirmed that this animal was a polar bear grizzly hybrid through DNA testing, and, the first hybrid found in the wild.

This bear appears to be the product of a polar bear mother and a grizzly bear father. Until 2006, there had been no documented cases of a grizzly polar bear hybrid found in the wild.

12. Which grizzly bear features did the hybrid bear have?

    a. Brown patches in certain areas

    b. Long claws

    c. A shallow face

    d. All of the above

13. The hybrid bear was the result of

    a. A male brown bear and a female grizzly.

    b. A female brown bear and a male grizzly bear.

    c. A female polar bear and a male grizzly bear.

    d. A male polar bear and a female grizzly.

14. The hybrid bear tested in this case was

    a. The first case ever known where two different bear species mated successfully.

    b. Genetically flawed and prone to many diseases and conditions.

    c. A fluke, and a mistake of nature which has never happened.

    d. The first proof of a wild bear hybrid species outside of zoos.

15. Modern science

   a. Has proven that the cubs from two different species will not survive in almost every case.

   b. Has known for some time that these hybrid bears were possible.

   c. Completely understands how bear hybrids occur and why this happens in nature.

   d. Has studied hundreds of bear hybrids in an attempt to learn more.

Strategy 5 - Elimination

For every question, no matter what type, eliminating obviously incorrect answers narrows the possible choices. Elimination is probably the most powerful strategy for answering multiple-choice.

Directions: Read the passage below, and answer the questions using this strategy.

Peacocks have been admired throughout history for their beautiful plumage and train of the male peafowl, or peacock, with its characteristic eye pattern.

In Greek mythology, Hera, wife of Zuess, and queen of the Gods, placed the hundred eyes of the slain giant Argus on the tail of the peacock, her favorite bird.

The peacock's tail or train, is not actually the tail, but the elongated feathers of the upper tail. These beautiful green-bronze feathers, with the eye pattern, can be seen when the train is fanned out. The actual tail feathers of the peacock are short and grey-colored and can be seen from behind when the train is fanned in a courtship display.

The grey tail feathers can also be seen during molting season, when males drop the feathers in their train. The female peacock is duller compared to the spectacular male. The female is brown, with some green iridescence feathers on her neck.

16. The long colorful tail feathers of the peacock

    a. Are only present in the male of the species

    b. Are used by both sexes to warn off predators

    c. Are normally red and blue in color

    d. Are only present for a very short time each year

17. The differences between the male and female peacock are

    a. Size and weight

    b. Coloring and tail feather length

    c. The female does not ever leave the nest

    d. The male sits on and hatches the eggs

18. The term peacock actually refers to

    a. Both sexes from the pheasant family

    b. The eyes on the tail feathers of the bird

    c. The male bird of the peafowl species

    d. The female bird of the peafowl species

19. The gray tail feathers on the male peacock can be seen

    a. When the bird is startled

    b. Only when the bird is searching for food

    c. When the peacock lowers the tail feathers to the ground

    d. During molting

Strategy 6 - Opposites

For every question, no matter what type, look at answers that are opposites. When two answers are opposites, the odds increase that one of them is the correct answer.

Directions: Read the passage below, and answer the questions using this strategy.

Smallpox is a highly infectious disease unique to humans, caused by two virus, Variola Major and Minor. The Latin name for smallpox is Variola or Variola Vera, which means spotted.

In 1980, the World Health Organization certified that Smallpox had been eradicated. Smallpox is sometimes confused with Chicken Pox, however, they are different virus.

The smallpox virus lives in the small blood vessels in the mouth, throat and skin. This gives a distinct rash in these areas, which turn into blisters. After being exposed to the Smallpox virus, symptoms do not appear for 12 to 17 days.

Variola Major is much more serious virus, with a mortality rate of 30 – 35%. Variola Minor is milder, with a mortality rate of only 1%. Variola Minor has a number of common names, including, alastrim, cottonpox, milkpox, whitepox, and Cuban itch.

Variola Major causes several long-term complications such as scars, commonly on the face, which occurs in about 65 – 85% of the survivors. Other complications, including blindness and deformities from arthritis and other complications are much less common, about 2 – 5%.

20. Smallpox

    a. Effects all mammals, including humans

    b. Is caused by a bacteria from contact with dead flesh

    c. Was called the great pox during the fifteenth century

    d. Only affects humans, although other species can carry and transmit the virus

21. Smallpox caused by Variola major has a

   a. Thirty to thirty five percent survival rate

   b. Sixty percent mortality rate

   c. Thirty to thirty five percent mortality rate

   d. Sixty percent survival rate

22. Smallpox caused by Variola minor is

   a. Much more severe, with more pox and scarring

   b. Much less severe, with fewer pox and less scarring

   c. Characterized because there are no pox

   d. So minor that no treatment or medical attention is needed

23. Smallpox can be fatal

   a. In between thirty and thirty five percent of those who catch the virus, depending on the type

   b. In between thirty and sixty five percent of those who catch the virus, depending on the type

   c. When no medical treatment is available

   d. Only in developing countries where medical care is poor

Strategy 7 - Look for Differences

For every question, no matter what type, look at the two choices that seem to be correct and then examine the differences between the two. Refer to the stem to determine the best answer.

Directions: Read the passage below, and answer the questions using this strategy.

Lightning is one of the most amazing natural phenomenon. A popular belief is that lightning cannot strike twice in the same place. This however, is not true - lightning does strike in the same place frequently.

Lightning is an electrical discharge between clouds and the ground, or between two clouds. It is often accompanied with thunder during thunderstorms, dust storms and volcanic eruptions. Every year, there are an estimated 16 million lightning storms worldwide.

Bolts of lightning travel at speeds of 130,000 miles per hour and contain a billion volts of electricity. Lightning bolts can reach temperatures of 54,000° F. This is hot enough to turn sand, some soils or even rock into hollow glass channels, called fulgurites. Fulgurites extend far below the surface.

Lightning is such a common feature of the natural world, there is even a classification for the fear of lightning and thunder, called astraphobia.

Clouds of volcanic ash, as well as dust storms and forest fires can generate enough static electricity to produce lightning.

Scientists do not understand the process of lightning formation, and this is a matter for debate. Scientists have studied causes of lightning, such as wind, humidity, friction, atmospheric pressure, solar winds and accumulation of charged solar particles. Many scientists believe that ice inside clouds is important in causing lightning.

24. Astraphobia is

    a. Fear of thunder

    b. Fear of thunder and lightning

    c. Fear of lightning

    d. None of the above

25. Lightning occurs

    a. Only in thunderstorms

    b. In thunderstorms and dust storms

    c. In thunderstorms, volcanic eruptions and dust storms

    d. In the upper atmosphere

26. Fulgurites are

    a. Made of silica

    b. Made of glass

    c. Made of sand, soil and rock turned into glass

    d. Made of silica and glass

Strategy 8 - Context clues

Look at the sentences and the context to determine the best option. Sometimes, the answer may be located right in the passage or question.

Directions: Read the passage below, and answer the questions using this strategy.

Venus is one of the four solar terrestrial planets, or rocky bodies that orbit the sun. Planets are defined as a celestial body moving in an elliptical orbit around a star. Venus is about the same size as Earth. Venus' diameter (12,104 km) is only 650 km. less than Earth's, (12,742 km.) and its mass is 81.5% of Earth's. The Venusian atmosphere is a dense mixture of carbon dioxide with some nitrogen.

Venus orbits the sun every 224.7 days, and is the second-closest planet to the Sun.

Venus, as the second brightest star in the sky, after the moon, reaches an apparent magnitude of −4.6, was named after Venus, the goddess of love and beauty by the Romans. The Romans named all the brightest stars after their Gods and Goddesses. Venus is often called the Morning, or Evening Star. Venus reaches its maximum brightness before sunrise and after sunset

Venus is an inferior planet from Earth, meaning that it is closer to the sun: its elongation reaches a maximum of 47.8°.

27. Apparent magnitude is

    a. A measure of darkness

    b. A measure of brightness

    c. The distance from the moon

    d. The distance from the earth

28. The elongation of a planet is

    a. The angular distance from the sun, as seen from earth.

    b. The distance from the sun

    c. The distance form the earth

    d. None of the above

29. Terrestrial planets are

    a. Made of rock

    b. Have people on them

    c. The earth and no others

    d. The same size as Earth

30. How many planets orbit the sun in less than 224.7 days?

    a. 1 planet

    b. Only Venus

    c. 2 planets

    d. 3 planets

Strategy 9 - Try Every Option

For definition questions, try out all the options - one option will fit better than the rest. As you go through the options, use Strategy 5 - Elimination, to eliminate obviously incorrect choices as you go.

Directions: Read the passage below, and answer the questions using this strategy.

Some of the common weather patterns on Earth are rain, wind, fog, and snow. Other weather patterns, generally classified as natural disasters, are hurricanes, tornadoes, typhoons and ice storms. Weather generally happens in the lower portion of the atmosphere, called the troposphere. Some weather can occur in the upper atmosphere, or stratosphere, where it can effect weather in the lower troposphere.

The principle cause of weather is different temperature, barometric pressure and moisture densities in the atmosphere. Weather phenomena in the atmosphere such as the jet stream is caused by the temperature differences in the tropical and polar air, which causes air to move from one to the other. The jet stream generally flows in a Western direction, and there are two or three jet streams in the Northern and Southern Hemispheres at any time.

Instabilities in the flow of the jet stream cause weather systems such as extra-tropical cyclones. Different processes cause weather systems such as monsoons or thunderstorms. Monsoons are caused by a difference in temperature over land and over sea.

Due to the tilt of the Earth's axis, sunlight reaches the Earth at different angles at different times of the year, creating seasons. In January, the Northern Hemisphere is tilted away from the sun, so sunlight is more direct than in July.

31. The troposphere is

    a. The highest strata of the atmosphere

    b. The lowest strata of the atmosphere

    c. The middle level of the atmosphere

    d. Not part of the atmosphere

32. Monsoons are

    a. Caused by instabilities in the jet stream

    b. Caused by processes other than instabilities in the jet stream

    c. Part of the jet stream

    d. Cause the jet stream

33. Extra-tropical cyclones occur

    a. In the tropics

    b. In temperate zones

    c. In the gulf stream

    d. In mid-latitudes

34. Tilted means:

    a. Slanted

    b. Rotating

    c. Connected to

    d. Bent

Strategy 10 - Work for it

For questions about supporting details, work is the key. Review the passage to locate the right option. Never forget the choices that you are given are designed to confuse, and they may *seem* reasonable answers. However, if they are not mentioned in the text, they are "red herring" answers.

The best answer is the exact answer mentioned in the text.

Directions: Read the passage below, and answer the questions using this strategy.

Ebola is a common term for a group of viruses in the genus Ebola (EBOV), family Filoviridae. There are several species within the Ebola virus genus, with specific strains. Ebola is also a general term for the disease the viruses cause, Ebola hemorrhagic fever. The Ebola virus is transmitted through bodily fluids.

The Ebola virus interferes with the cell and patients die of hypovolemic shock.

The Ebola viruses are similar to the Marburg virus, also in the family Filoviridae. Most viruses are spherical, however, the Ebola viruses have long filaments. The Ebola and Marburg viruses have similar symptoms.

The first outbreak of Ebola occurred near the Ebola River, in the Democratic Republic of the Congo, which the disease and viruses are named after. Ebola is a very serious illness, very contagious and often fatal. The 2014 West African Ebola viral epidemic was the most widespread in history.

The Zaire virus was the first discovered in 1976 and is the most lethal. Ebola first emerged in 1976 in Zaire. An outbreak in Reston, Virginia brought the virus to international attention.

35. The Ebola virus received this name because of

       a. The doctor who first discovered the virus

       b. The cure that is used to treat those infected

       c. The river where the disease was first encountered

       d. What the virus does to the body

36. Viruses in the Ebola genus are recognizable

       a. Because of their hooked shape

       b. Because of their long filaments

       c. Due to their oblong heads

       d. Because of their unique color

37. One of the most common causes of death from the Ebola family of viruses is

    a. Hypovolemic shock due to blood vessel damage

    b. Bleeding of the brain that cannot be stopped

    c. A heart attack from blood loss and lack of fluids

    d. A high fever that cannot be lowered

38. The most deadly strain of the Ebola virus family is the

    a. The Reston strain

    b. The Ivory Coast strain

    c. The Zaire strain

    d. The Sudan strain

Strategy 11 - Look at the Big Picture

Details can be tricky when dealing with main idea and summary questions, but do not let the details distract you. Look at the big picture instead of the smaller parts to determine the right answer.

Directions: Read the passage below, and answer the questions using this strategy.

In 2005 researchers found three species of fruit bat carrying the Ebola virus, but not showing disease symptoms. These three species are called natural host, or reservoir species. Scientists have studied plants, insects and birds as potential reservoir species without success. Bats are the only reservoir species scientists have found. Apparently, bats are reservoir species for several viruses.

The first outbreaks, in 1976 and 1979, were in cotton factories where bats lived. Bats were also present in the Marburg infections in 1975 and 1980.

39. The species most suspected as a potential Ebola virus reservoir is

    a. Birds

    b. Insects

    c. Plants

    d. Bats

40. Most plant and animal species

    a. Can carry the Ebola virus but not become infected

    b. Can not carry and transmit the Ebola virus

    c. Are responsible for new cases of Ebola viruses

    d. Can be infected with one of the Ebola viruses

41. Bats are known for

    a. Being carriers of many different viruses, including Ebola

    b. Transmitting the Ebola virus through a scratch

    c. Being susceptible to the virus and becoming infected

    d. Transmitting the Ebola virus through infected droppings

Strategy 12 - Best Possible Answer

Try to determine the best possible answer according to the information given in the passage. Do not be distracted by answers that seem correct or are mostly correct.

Directions: Read the passage below, and answer the questions using this strategy.

Ebola may not be contagious initially but as the disease progresses, bodily fluids are extremely contagious.

Lack of proper equipment and proper hygiene has caused epidemics in poor and isolated areas. Unfortunately, infectious reservoirs generally exist in areas do not have modern hospitals or educated medical staff, adding to the chance of epidemics.

42. Ebola is highly contagious

a. Only when blood is present

b. Only in the first stages before hemorrhaging occurs

c. At all stages of the illness from incubation to recovery

d. Only in the later stages

43. Exposure to the Ebola virus means

a. A death sentence for most patients

b. Isolation for the patient, and proper precautions for all medical personnel to contain the virus

c. The virus will spread rapidly and there is no treatment available

d. A full recovery usually, with very few symptoms

44. Ebola outbreaks commonly occur

a. Because sterilization and containment procedures are not followed or available

b. Due to infected animals in the area

c. Because of rat droppings in homes

d. Because of a contaminated water supply

45. Ebola is

a. More common in advanced nations where treatment makes the disease minor

b. More common in third world and developing countries

c. Fatal in more than ninety-five percent of the cases

d. Highly contagious during the incubation period

Answers to Sample Multiple-Choice Strategy Questions

Strategy 1 - Keywords in the question tell what the question is asking

1. B
The question asks about the free range *method* of farming. Here method refers to *type* of farming. "Method" here is the keyword and can be marked or underlined.

2. D
The Question is, "Free-range farming is *practiced* ..." The keyword here is "practiced." Looking at the choices, which all start with "to," it is clear the answer will be about *why* free range ... Also notice that one choice is "All of the above," which in this case is the correct answer. However, when "All of the above" is an option, this is a potential Elimination Strategy. All you have to do is find one choice that is incorrect and you can use Strategy 5 - Elimination to eliminate two choices and increase your odds from one in four, to one in two.

3. A
The question is, "Free range farming husbandry ..." From the question, and the *lack* of keywords, together with the choices presented, the answer will be a definition free range farming husbandry.

4. C
The question is, "Free-range certification is *most important* to farmers because ... " The keywords here are "most important." Circle the keywords to keep them clear in your mind. Be careful to choose the best possible answer.

Strategy 2 - Negatives

These four questions all have negatives: does not mean, is never, do not, and is not. These questions exclude possibilities, so if you see any choices that are true, you can eliminate them right away.

5. D

The question asks what sexual dimorphism does *not* mean. Circle the word "not" and keep it firmly in mind. Next, what is sexual dimorphism. Reading the text quickly, sexual dimorphism is related to the female bears being smaller than the males. Probably there are other aspects, but this general definition is all that is needed to answer the question.

First, notice that "All of the above" is choice D. In addition, the question is a negative. So, for choice D to be correct, choices A, B and C must be *in*correct. This narrows down your options. If any of choices A, B or C are correct, then you can eliminate that choice as well as choice D.

Either all the choices are *in*correct, in which case, choice D, "All of the above" is correct.

Choice A, male and females are the same size is incorrect. Choice B, all grizzly bears look the same and are the same size, is incorrect. Choice C, grizzly bears (plural so *all* grizzly bears) can be large and weigh more than half a ton. This is incorrect since while all grizzly bears are large, female bears weight less than half a ton.

All three choices are incorrect so choice D is the correct answer, "All of the Above," are incorrect.

6. A

First, circle or underline never to show this is a negative question. Now look at the options to find an option that is not true.

Choice A is true as male bears are 1,000 pounds. Place a mark beside this one. It may be tempting to select this option as your answer, but it is important to look at all choices before making a final decision.

Choice B is not true - size does not depend on the sex.
Choice C is not true - size does not depend on diet.
Choice D is not true - males often stand 8 feet.

So choice A is correct.

7. A

First circle "do not" to mark this as a negative question.

Choice A is correct, Yukon River grizzly bears do not get as big as other grizzlies, so put a mark beside it for later consideration. Examine the other choices before making a final decision.

Choice B is not mentioned in the text, and can be eliminated.

Choice C is not mentioned in the text and can be eliminated.

Choice D is true, but this is a negative question so it is false.

Some of the above choices may be true from a common sense point of view, but if they aren't mentioned specifically in the passage, they can be eliminated.

Choice A is correct.

Strategy 3 - Read the Stem Completely

Read the question, and then look for the answer in the text before reading the choices. Reading the choices first will confuse, just as it is meant to do! Do not fall into this trap!

8. B
The choices here are very confusing and are meant to be! Four variations on the latin species name, Ursus Arctos are given, so the question is what version of this latin name is correct, which gives a very straight-forward strategy to solving. Since the name is latin, it is going to stand out in the text. Take the first option, "Arctas Ursinas," and scan the text for something that looks like that. At the end of the second sentence is "Ursus Arctos," which is very close. Next confirm what this sentence refers to, which gives the correct answer, Choice B.

9. D
This question asks why Kodiak brown bears are a different subspecies, and the options are designed to confuse a careless, stressed test-taker. Scan the text for "Kodiak," which appears in the second to last sentence, and answers the question.

10. C
This question asks about the relationship between brown bears and grizzly bears. If you are not careful you will be confused by the choices.

11. A
Read the question, then read the text before trying to answer and avoid confusion.

Strategy 4 - Consider all choices before deciding

In Strategy 3, we learned to find the correct answer in the text before reading the choices. Now you have read the text and have the right answer. The next thing is Strategy 4 - Read *all* the choices. Once you have read all the choices, select the correct choice.

12. D
First, notice that "All of the above" is a choice. So if you find one option that is incorrect, you can eliminate that option and option D, "All of the above." Reading the question first, (Strategy #3) then looking in the text, and then reading all the choices before answering, you can see that choices A, B and C are all correct, so choice D, All of the Above, is the correct choice.
If you had not read all the choices first, then you might be tempted to impulsively choose A, B, or C.

13. C
Looking at the choices, they are designed to confuse with different choices and combinations. Recognizing this, it is therefore important to be extra careful in making your choice. If you are stressed, in a hurry, or not paying attention, you will probably get this question wrong by making an impulsive choice and not reading through all the choices before making a selection.

Referring to the text, you will find the sentence, "... it was a hybrid, with the mother a polar bear and the father a grizzly," which answers the question.

14. D
Reading through all the choices, B and C can be eliminated right away as they are not mentioned in the text. They might appear as good answers but they are not from the passage.

Looking at choices A and D, the issue is if this has happened before, or has it happened only in zoos. Referring to the text, the second paragraph tells us it is the first hybrid found in the wild.

15. B
Reading through the four choices, the question concerns, what does science know? Does it happen all the time? Completely understood? They do survive? Is it possible? Look in the text for how much is known. The last sentence, "Until 2006, there had been no documented cases of a grizzly polar bear hybrid found in the wild." gives the answer.

Strategy 5 - Elimination.

For every question, no matter what type, eliminating obviously incorrect answers narrows the possible choices. Elimination is probably the most powerful strategy for answering multiple-choice.

16. A
Using this strategy the choices can be narrowed down to choices A and D. I have never seen a peacock with red in their tail, so choice C can *probably* be eliminated, but check back. Most birds and many animals have a pattern where the male is colorful and the female less colorful. Choice B can be eliminated as it refers to "both sexes" having colorful tails. Choice D is a good candidate as the text refers to molting season, however, the text does not say how long this is, so there is some doubt. This makes choice A the best choice as it is referred to directly in the text.

17. B
Choice D can be eliminated right away, as a male bird to sit on eggs is not mentioned in the text.

Skimming the passage, choices A and C can be eliminated, as they are not mentioned directly in the text, leaving only choice D.

18. C
Choices A, B and D can be eliminated right away, as the passage states the peacock is the male bird. Referring to the text, "plumage and train of the male peafowl, or peacock ..." making choice C the best choice.

19. D
Choices A and B can be eliminated either right away or with a quick check of the passage, since they are not mentioned. Choice C is suspicious since the grey feathers are under the tail feathers, so it is difficult to see how they could be visible when the tail feathers are lowered.

Strategy 6 - Opposites

If there are opposites, one of them is generally the correct answer. If it helps, make a table that lays out the different options and the correct option will become clear.

20. D
Notice that choices A and D are opposites. Referring to the text, "Smallpox is a highly infectious disease unique to humans ..." eliminates choice A. Also notice choices B and C are not mentioned in the text and can be eliminated right away.

21. C
Notice that all the choices are opposites. 30% - 35% mortality, or survival rate, or 60%. Therefore, the task is to review the text, looking for 30% or 60%, survival or mortality, stay clear, and do not get confused. Sometimes making notes or a table can help to clarify.

The question is asking about percent, so it is easy and fast to skim the passage for a percent sign.

The first percent sign is in the fourth paragraph, 30% - 35%. Write this in the margin. Next, see what this percent refers to, which is the mortality rate. Write "mortality" next to 30% - 35%. Now, working backwards, see what the 30% - 35% mortality rate refers to. At the beginning of that sentence, is Variola Major.

30% - 35%	Mortality	V. Major

Now we have a clear understanding of what the passage is saying, which we have retrieved quickly and easily, and hopefully will not be confused by the different choices.

Choices A and B can be eliminated right away. Choice C looks correct. Check choice D quickly, and confirm that it is incorrect. Choice C is the correct answer.

22. B
Choices A and B are opposites. Is Variola Minor more or less severe, with more or fewer pox, and more or less scarring? The other two choices, "no pox" and "no treatment" can be eliminated quickly. Either choice A or B are going to be wrong.

Make a quick table like this:

Major - more serious - scars, blindness
Minor - milder

The passage does not mention scarring from Variola minor, but we can infer that it is milder. Looking at the options, choice A is clearly talking about Variola major, and we can infer that choice B is talking about Variola minor and is the correct answer. We can confirm our inference from the text.

Also note the words, 'major' and 'minor.' Which gives a clue concerning severity, and the elimination of choice A.

23. A
Choices A and B are not exactly opposite, but very close and designed to confuse if you do not read them properly. How many people die from the virus? Between 30% and 35%? Or between 35% and 60%? Scan the text with these numbers in mind.

This question is asking about a percent, so quickly scan the passage for a percent sign, which first appears in the second paragraph. Working back, confirm that the percent figures that you quickly found is related to mortality, which it is.

Strategy 7 - Look for Differences.

Look at two choices that appear to be correct and examine them carefully.

24. B
Choices A, B and C are very similar and designed to confuse and distract someone who does not look carefully at the text. What is astraphobia exactly? This is a definition question for an unusual word, astraphobia. Scan the text for "astraphobia." Choice B is correct.

25. C
Choices A, B and C are similar and designed to confuse, or tempt a stressed or careless test-taker into making a quick and incorrect choice. Checking the passage, in the first paragraph, lightning occurs in thunderstorms, volcanic eruptions and in dust storms, so choice C is correct.

26. C
All four answers are similar and designed to confuse. Seeing how similar the choices are, it is very important to be clear on the exact definition. Scan the text quickly for the word "fulgurites." From the third paragraph, "This is hot enough to turn sand, some soils or even rock into hollow glass channels..." so the correct answer, and the option that answers the question best, is choice C.

Strategy 8 - Context clues.

Look at the sentences and the context to determine the best option. Sometimes, the answer may be located right in the passage or question.

27. B
You do not have to know the exact meaning - just enough to answer the question. The phrase is used in the passage, "Venus, as the second brightest star in the sky, after the moon, reaches an apparent magnitude of −4.6 ..." where Venus is compared to the brightness of the moon, so the apparent magnitude must have something to do with brightness, which is enough information to answer the question. Notice also, how the choices are opposites. Choice A and B are opposites as are choices C and D.

28. A
The exact meaning is not necessary, you only need only enough information to answer the question. The passage where this phrase is used is, "Venus is an inferior planet from Earth, meaning that it is closer to the sun: its elongation reaches a maximum of 47.8°." Elongation in this sentence is something connected with distance from the sun, but also something to do with Earth. Choice C can be eliminated right away, and since one choice is wrong, Choice D, All of the Above, can also be eliminated. Choice A is the best answer since it mentions, "as seen from earth."

29. A
Choices C and D can be eliminated right away. No mention is made of size or people, so choices C and D are also incorrect. Terrestrial has many similar meanings, but choice A is the best. From the passage, "Venus is one of the four solar terrestrial planets, or rocky bodies that orbit the sun."

Note that choice B is a grammatical error and can be eliminated right away. The question is, "Terrestrial planets are," and choice B is, "Have people on them."

This is a great strategy, looking for grammatical errors and eliminating, and what you might expect to see on a test that a professor has made themselves. However, most standardized tests are generated by computer, and proofed by many different people who have considerable expertise in correcting this type of easy question. Keep this in mind because it is an easy elimination, but don't expect to see this type of thing on a standardized test.

30. A
This is a bit of a trick question and designed to confuse, as it requires an additional step of logical reasoning. Referring to the text, Venus is the *second* closest planet to the sun so there must be one planet that is closer. Planets closer to the sun will rotate the sun faster, so the answer must be choice A.

Strategy 9 - Try out every option for word meaning questions.

For definition questions, try out all the options - one option will fit better than the rest. As you go through the options, use Strategy 5 - Elimination, to eliminate obviously incorrect choices as you go.

31. B
The answer is taken directly from the passage. Notice that choices A and B are opposites, so one of them will be incorrect. Look in the text carefully for the exact definition. If you are uncertain, make a table in the margin.

Scan the passage looking for the word you are asked to define. Large or unusual words generally stand out and can be located quickly. Once you have found the position in the passage of the word using quick reading scanning techniques, then focus on the sentence and read carefully.

32. B
The sentences talking about the jet stream and monsoons are next to one another. Trying each definition, and comparing to the text, only choice B fits. If you are uncertain, copy the information from the passage into a table.

The question is, what is the relationship between monsoons and the jet stream.

Scan the passage for "jet stream" and "monsoon."

Tropical cyclones	Jet stream
Monsoons and thunderstorms	Different processes

33. D
Referring to the passage, and trying each definition choice, choice D is the only answer that makes sense referring to the text.

34. A
The passage from the text is, "Due to the tilt of the Earth's axis, sunlight reaches the Earth at different angles at differ-

ent times of the year, creating seasons." Substituting all the choices given into this sentence, slanted, choice A, is the only sensible answer. Here is what substitutions look like:

> a. In June the Northern Hemisphere is *slanted* towards the sun...
>
> b. In June the Northern Hemisphere is *rotating* towards the sun...
>
> c. In June the Northern Hemisphere is *connected to* towards the sun...
>
> d. In June the Northern Hemisphere is *bent* towards the sun...

Choice A is the only one that makes sense.

Strategy 10 - You have to work for it! Check carefully for supporting details.

All answers can be found by carefully reading the text. The questions paraphrase the text found in the passage.

35. C
The passage has a lot of details so read carefully and stay clear.

36. B
The choices are designed to confuse. Check the text for the exact definition and do not be distracted by other choices.

37. A
Here is a quick tip. On choice A, the word hypovolemic is used. This is an unusual word and specific medical vocabulary. None of the other choices uses any specific vocabulary like this, so it is very likely to be the right answer. You can quickly scan the text for this word to confirm. Scanning the text for an unusual word is easy and fast, and one of the most powerful techniques for this type of question.

38. C
Scan the text for Zaire.

Strategy 11 - Look at the big picture

Details can be tricky when dealing with main idea and summary questions, but do not let the details distract you. Look at the big picture instead of the smaller parts to determine the right answer.

39. D
The passage says in 2005 it was found there are 3 fruit bat species most suspected of carrying the virus. The details (3 species, fruit bats and 2005) do not matter. Only the fact that bats are suspected.

40. B
The relevant passage is, "Scientists have studied plants, insects and birds as potential reservoir species without success. Bats are the only reservoir species scientists have found." The inference is that these plant and animal species cannot be infected, (i.e. carry and transmit the disease) so choice B is correct.

41. A
The relevant passage is, Apparently, bats are reservoir species for a number of viruses.

Strategy 12 - Make the best choice based on the information given.

42. D
Choices B and C are incorrect by the passage, "In the early stages, Ebola may not be highly contagious." Choice A is not mentioned, leaving choice D.

43. B
Choices A and D are obviously incorrect and can be eliminated right away. Choice C is irrelevant to the question.

44. A
Choices B and C are not mentioned in the passage. Choice D is a good possibility, however, choice A covers choice D and is referred to in the passage.

45. B
Choice A is incorrect. Choices C and D are not mentioned.

Practice Questions Answer Sheet

	A	B	C	D	E		A	B	C	D	E
1	○	○	○	○	○	21	○	○	○	○	○
2	○	○	○	○	○	22	○	○	○	○	○
3	○	○	○	○	○	23	○	○	○	○	○
4	○	○	○	○	○	24	○	○	○	○	○
5	○	○	○	○	○
6	○	○	○	○	○
7	○	○	○	○	○
8	○	○	○	○	○
9	○	○	○	○	○
10	○	○	○	○	○
11	○	○	○	○	○
12	○	○	○	○	○
13	○	○	○	○	○
14	○	○	○	○	○
15	○	○	○	○	○
16	○	○	○	○	○
17	○	○	○	○	○
18	○	○	○	○	○
19	○	○	○	○	○
20	○	○	○	○	○

Reading Comprehension Practice Questions

Questions 1 - 4 refer to the following passage.

Passage 1: "If You Have Allergies, You're Not Alone"

People who experience allergies might joke that their immune systems have let them down or are seriously lacking. Truthfully though, people who experience allergic reactions or allergy symptoms during certain times of the year have heightened immune systems that are, "better" than those of people who have perfectly healthy but less militant immune systems.

Still, when a person has an allergic reaction, they are having an adverse reaction to a substance that is considered normal to most people. Mild allergic reactions usually have symptoms like itching, runny nose, red eyes, or bumps or discoloration of the skin. More serious allergic reactions, such as those to animal and insect poisons or certain foods, may result in the closing of the throat, swelling of the eyes, low blood pressure, an inability to breathe, and can even be fatal.

Different treatments help different allergies, and which one a person uses depends on the nature and severity of the allergy. It is recommended to patients with severe allergies to take extra precautions, such as carrying an EpiPen, which treats anaphylactic shock and may prevent death, always in order for the remedy to be readily available and more effective. When an allergy is not so severe, treatments may be used just relieve a person of uncomfortable symptoms. Over the counter allergy medicines treat milder symptoms, and can be bought at any grocery store and used in moderation to help people with allergies live normally.

There are many tests available to assess whether a person has allergies or what they may be allergic to, and advances in these tests and the medicine used to treat patients continues to improve. Despite this fact, allergies still affect many people throughout the year or even every day. Medicines used to treat allergies have side effects of their own, and it is difficult to bring the body into balance with the use of medicine. Regardless, many of those who live with allergies are grateful for what is available and find it useful in maintaining their lifestyles.

1. According to this passage, the word "militant" belongs in a group with the words:

    a. sickly, ailing, faint

    b. strength, power, vigor

    c. active, fighting, warring

    d. worn, tired, breaking down

2. The author says that "medicines used to treat allergies have side effects of their own" to

    a. point out that doctors aren't very good at diagnosing and treating allergies

    b. argue that because of the large number of people with allergies, a cure will never be found

    c. explain that allergy medicines aren't cures and some compromise must be made

    d. argue that more wholesome remedies should be researched and medicines banned

3. It can be inferred that _____ recommend that some people with allergies carry medicine with them.

    a. the author

    b. doctors

    c. the makers of EpiPen

    d. people with allergies

4. The author has written this passage to

    a. inform readers on symptoms of allergies so people with allergies can get help

    b. persuade readers to be proud of having allergies

    c. inform readers on different remedies so people with allergies receive the right help

    d. describe different types of allergies, their symptoms, and their remedies

Questions 5 - 8 refer to the following passage.

Passage 2: "When a Poet Longs to Mourn, He Writes an Elegy"

Poems are an expressive, especially emotional, form of writing. They have been present in literature virtually from the time civilizations invented the written word. Poets often portrayed as moody, secluded, and even troubled, but this is because poets are introspective and feel deeply about the current events and cultural norms they are surrounded with. Poets often produce the most telling literature, giving insight into the society and mind-set they come from. This can be done in many forms.

The oldest types of poems often include many stanzas, may or may not rhyme, and are more about telling a story than experimenting with language or words. The most common types of ancient poetry are epics, which are usually extremely long stories that follow a hero through his journey, or elegies, which are often solemn in tone and used to mourn or lament something or someone. The Mesopotamians are often said to have invented the written word, and their literature is among the oldest in the world, including the epic poem titled "Epic of Gilgamesh". Similar in style and length to "Gilgamesh" is "Beowulf", an elegy poem written in Old English and set in Scandinavia. These poems are often used by professors as the earliest examples of literature.

The importance of poetry was revived in the Renaissance. At

this time, Europeans discovered the style and beauty of ancient Greek arts, and poetry was among those. Shakespeare is the most well-known poet of the time, and he used poetry not only to write poems but also to write plays for the theater. The most popular forms of poetry during the Renaissance included villanelles (a nineteen-line poem with two rhymes throughout), sonnets, as well as the epic. Poets during this time focused on style and form, and developed very specific rules and outlines for how an exceptional poem should be written.

As often happens in the arts, modern poets have rejected the constricting rules of Renaissance poets, and free form poems are much more popular. Some modern poems would read just like stories if they weren't arranged into lines and stanzas. It is difficult to tell which poems and poets will be the most important, because works of art often become more famous in hindsight, after the poet has died and society can look at itself without being in the moment. Modern poetry continues to develop, and will no doubt continue to change as values, thought, and writing continue to change.

Poems can be among the most enlightening and uplifting texts for a person to read if they are looking to connect with the past, connect with other people, or try to gain an understanding of what is happening in their time.

5. In summary, the author has written this passage

    a. as a foreword that will introduce a poem in a book or magazine

    b. because she loves poetry and wants more people to like it

    c. to give a brief history of poems

    d. to convince students to write poems

6. The author organizes the paragraphs mainly by

    a. moving chronologically, explaining which types of poetry were common in that time

    b. talking about new types of poems each paragraph and explaining them a little

    c. focusing on one poet or group of people and the poems they wrote

    d. explaining older types of poetry so she can talk about modern poetry

7. The author's claim that poetry has been around "virtually from the time civilizations invented the written word" is supported by the detail that

    a. Beowulf is written in Old English, which is not really in use any longer

    b. epic poems told stories about heroes

    c. the Renaissance poets tried to copy Greek poets

    d. the Mesopotamians are credited with both inventing the word and writing "Epic of Gilgamesh"

8. According to the passage, the word "telling" means

    a. speaking

    b. significant

    c. soothing

    d. wordy

Questions 9 - 12 refer to the following passage.

Passage 3: "Winged Victory of Samothrace: the Statue of the Gods"

Students who read about the "Winged Victory of Samothrace" probably won't be able to picture what this statue looks like. However, almost anyone who knows a little about statues will recognize it when they see it: it is the statue of a winged woman who does not have arms or a head. Even the most famous pieces of art may be recognized by sight but not by name.

This iconic statue is of the Greek goddess Nike, who represented victory and was called Victoria by the Romans. The statue is sometimes called the "Nike of Samothrace". She was often displayed in Greek art as driving a chariot, and her speed or efficiency with the chariot may be what her wings symbolize. It is said that the statue was created around 200 BCE to celebrate a battle that was won at sea. Archaeologists and art historians believe the statue may have originally been part of a temple or other building, even one of the most important temples, Megaloi Theoi, just as many statues were used during that time.

"Winged Victory" does indeed appear to have had arms and a head when it was originally created, and it is unclear why they were removed or lost. Indeed, they have never been discovered, even with all the excavation that has taken place. Many speculate that one of her arms was raised and put to her mouth, as though she was shouting or calling out, which is consistent with the idea of her as a war figure. If the missing pieces were ever to be found, they might give Greek and art historians more of an idea of what Nike represented or how the statue was used. Learning about pieces of art through details like these can help students remember time frames or locations, as well as learn about the people who occupied them.

9. The author's title says the statue is "of the Gods" because

      a. the statue is very beautiful and even a god would find it beautiful

      b. the statue is of a Greek goddess, and gods were of primary importance to the Greek

      c. Nike lead the gods into war

      d. the statues were used at the temple of the gods and so it belonged to them

10. The third paragraph states that

a. the statue is related to war and was probably broken apart by foreign soldiers

b. the arms and head of the statue cannot be found because all the excavation has taken place

c. speculations have been made about what the entire statue looked like and what it symbolized

d. the statue has no arms or head because the sculptor lost them

11. The author's main purpose in writing this passage is to

a. demonstrate that art and culture are related and one can teach us about the other

b. persuade readers to become archeologists and find the missing pieces of the statue

c. teach readers about the Greek goddess Nike

d. to teach readers the name of a statue they probably recognize

12. The author specifies the indirect audience as "students" because

a. it is probably a student who is taking this test

b. most young people don't know much about art yet and most young people are students

c. students read more than people who are not students

d. the passage is based on a discussion of what we can learn about culture from art

Questions 13 - 16 refer to the following passage.

Passage 4: "Ways Characters Communicate in Theater"

Playwrights give their characters voices in a way that gives depth and added meaning to what happens on stage during their play. There are different types of speech in scripts that allow characters to talk with themselves, with other characters, and even with the audience.

It is very unique to theater that characters may talk "to themselves." When characters do this, the speech they give is called a soliloquy. Soliloquies are usually poetic, introspective, moving, and can tell audience members about the feelings, motivations, or suspicions of an individual character without that character having to reveal them to other characters on stage. "To be or not to be" is a famous soliloquy given by Hamlet as he considers difficult but important themes, such as life and death.

The most common type of communication in plays is when one character is speaking to another or a group of other characters. This is generally called dialogue, but can also be called monologue if one character speaks without being interrupted for a long time. It is not necessarily the most important type of communication, but it is the most common because the plot of the play cannot really progress without it.

Lastly, and most unique to theater (although it has been used somewhat in film) is when a character speaks directly to the audience. This is called an aside, and scripts usually specifically direct actors to do this. Asides are usually comical, an inside joke between the character and the audience, and very short. The actor will usually face the audience when delivering them, even if it's for a moment, so the audience can recognize this move as an aside.

All three of these types of communication are important to the art of theater, and have been perfected by famous playwrights like Shakespeare. Understanding these types of communication can help an audience member grasp what is artful about the script and action of a play.

13. According to the passage, characters in plays communicate to

    a. move the plot forward

    b. show the private thoughts and feelings of one character

    c. make the audience laugh

    d. add beauty and artistry to the play

14. When Hamlet delivers "To be or not to be", he can most likely be described as

    a. solitary

    b. thoughtful

    c. dramatic

    d. hopeless

15. The author uses parentheses to punctuate "although it has been used somewhat in film"

    a. to show that films are less important

    b. instead of using commas so that the sentence is not interrupted

    c. because parenthesis help separate details that are not as important

    d. to show that films are not as artistic

16. by the phrase "give their characters voices," the author means that

    a. playwrights are generous

    b. playwrights are changing the sound or meaning of characters' voices to fit what they had in mind

    c. dialogue is important in creating characters

    d. playwrights may be the parent of one of their actors and literally give them their voice

Questions 17 - 20 refer to the following passage.

Passage 5: "Women and Advertising"

Only in the last few generations have media messages been so widespread and so readily seen, heard, and read by so many people. Advertising is an important part of both selling and buying anything from soap to cereal to jeans. For whatever reason, more consumers are women than are men. Media message are subtle but powerful, and more attention has been paid lately to how these message affect women.

Of all the products that women buy, makeup, clothes, and other stylistic or cosmetic products are among the most popular. This means that companies focus their advertising on women, promising them that their product will make her feel, look, or smell better than the next company's product will. This competition has resulted in advertising that is more and more ideal and less and less possible for everyday women. However, because women do look to these ideals and the products they represent as how they can potentially become, many women have developed unhealthy attitudes about themselves when they have failed to become those ideals.

In recent years, more companies have tried to change advertisements to be healthier for women. This includes featuring models of more sizes and addressing a huge outcry against unfair tools such as airbrushing and photo editing. There is debate about what the right balance between real and ideal is, because fashion is also considered art and some changes are made to purposefully elevate fashionable products and signify that they are creative, innovative, and the work of individual people. Artists want their freedom protected as much as women do, and advertising agencies are often caught in the middle.

Some claim that the companies who make these changes are not doing enough. Many people worry that there are still not enough models of different sizes and different ethnicities. Some people claim that companies use this healthier type of advertisement not for the good of women, but because they would like to sell products to the women who are looking for these kinds of messages. This is also a hard balance to find: companies do need to make money, and women do need to feel respected.

While the focus of this change has been on women, advertising can also affect men, and this change will hopefully be a lesson on media for all consumers.

17. The second paragraph states that advertising focuses on women

    a. to shape what the ideal should be

    b. because women buy makeup

    c. because women are easily persuaded

    d. because of the types of products that women buy

18. According to the passage, fashion artists and female consumers are at odds because

    a. there is a debate going on and disagreement drives people apart

    b. both of them are trying to protect their freedom to do something

    c. artists want to elevate their products above the reach of women

    d. women are creative, innovative, individual people

19. The author uses the phrase "for whatever reason" in this passage to

    a. keep the focus of the paragraph on media messages and not on the differences between men and women

    b. show that the reason for this is unimportant

    c. argue that it is stupid that more women are consumers than men

    d. show that he or she is tired of talking about why media messages are important

20. This passage suggests that

    a. advertising companies are still working on making their messages better

    b. all advertising companies seek to be more approachable for women

    c. women are only buying from companies that respect them

    d. artists could stop producing fashionable products if they feel bullied

Questions 21 - 24 refer to the following passage.

Passage 6: "FDR, the Treaty of Versailles, and the Fourteen Points"

At the conclusion of World War I, both who had won the war and those who were forced to admit defeat welcomed the end of the war and anticipated that a peace treaty would be signed. The American president, Franklin Roosevelt, played an important part in proposing what the agreements should be and did so through his Fourteen Points.

World War I had begun in 1914 when an Austrian archduke was assassinated, leading to a domino effect that pulled the world's most powerful countries into war on a large scale. The war catalyzed the creation and use of deadly weapons that had not previously existed, resulting in a great loss of soldiers on both sides of the fighting. More than 9 million soldiers were killed.

The United States agreed to enter the war right before it ended, and they believed that its decision to become finally involved brought on the end of the war. FDR made it very clear that the U.S. was entering the war for moral reasons and had an agenda focused on world peace. The Fourteen Points were individual goals and ideas (focused on peace, free trade, open communication, and self-reliance) that FDR wanted the power nations to strive for now that the war had concluded.

He was optimistic and had many ideas about what could be accomplished through and during the post-war peace. However, FDR's fourteen points were poorly received when he presented them to the leaders of other world powers, many of whom wanted only to help their own countries and to punish the Germans for fueling the war, and they fell by the wayside. World War II was imminent, for Germany lost everything.

Some historians believe that the other leaders who participated in the Treaty of Versailles weren't receptive to the Fourteen Points because World War I was fought almost entirely on European soil, and the United States lost much less than did the other powers. FDR was in a unique position to help determine the fate of the war, but doing it on his own terms did not help accomplish his goals. This is only one historical example of how the United State has tried to use its power as an important country, but found itself limited because of geological or ideological factors.

21. The main idea of this passage is that

    a. World War I was unfair because no fighting took place in America

    b. World War II happened because of the Treaty of Versailles

    c. the power the United States has to help other countries also prevents it from helping other countries

    d. Franklin Roosevelt was one of the United States' smartest presidents

22. According to the second paragraph, World War I started because

    a. an archduke was assassinated

    b. weapons that were more deadly had been developed

    c. a domino effect of allies agreeing to help

    d. the world's most powerful countries were large

23. The author includes the detail that 9 million soldiers were killed

    a. to demonstrate why European leaders were hesitant to accept peace

    b. to show the reader the dangers of deadly weapons

    c. to make the reader think about which countries lost the most soldiers

    d. to demonstrate why World War II was imminent

24. According to this passage, the word catalyzed means

    a. analyzed

    b. sped up

    c. invented

    d. funded

Answer Key

Passage 1: "If You Have Allergies, You're Not Alone"

1. C
This question tests the reader's vocabulary skills. The uses of the negatives "but" and "less," especially right next to each other, may confuse readers into answering with choices A or D, which list words that are antonyms of "militant." Readers may also be confused by the comparison of healthy people with what is being described as an overly healthy person--both people are good, but the reader may look for which one is "worse" in the comparison, and therefore stray toward the antonyms. One key to understanding the meaning of "militant" if the reader is unfamiliar with it is to look at the root of the word; readers can then easily associate it with "military" and gain a sense of what the word signifies: defense (especially considered that the immune system defends the body). Choice C is correct over choice B because "militant" is an adjective, just as the words in C are, whereas the words in B are nouns.

2. C
This question tests the reader's understanding of function within writing. The other choices are details included surrounding the quoted text, and may therefore confuse the reader. A somewhat contradicts what is said earlier in the paragraph, which is that tests and treatments are improving, and probably doctors are along with them, but the paragraph doesn't actually mention doctors, and the subject of the question is the medicine. Choice B may seem correct to readers who aren't careful to understand that, while the author does mention the large number of people affected, the author is touching on the realities of living with allergies rather about the likelihood of curing all allergies. Similarly, while the author does mention the "balance" of the body, which is easily associated with "wholesome," the author is not really making an argument and especially is not making an extreme statement that allergy medicines should be outlawed. Again, because the article's tone is on living with allergies, choice C is an appropriate choice that fits with the title and content of the text.

3. B
This question tests the reader's inference skills. The text does not state who is doing the recommending, but the use of the "patients," as well as the general context of the passage, lends itself to the logical partner, "doctors," B. The author does mention the recommendation but doesn't present it as her own (i.e. "I recommend that"), so A may be eliminated. It may seem plausible that people with allergies (D) may recommend medicines or products to other people with allergies, but the text does not necessarily support this interaction taking place. Choice C may be selected because the EpiPen is specifically mentioned, but the use of the phrase "such as" when it is introduced is not limiting enough to assume the recommendation is coming from its creators.

4. D
This question tests the reader's global understanding of the text. Choice D includes the main topics of the three body paragraphs, and isn't too focused on a specific aspect or quote from the text, as the other questions are, giving a skewed summary of what the author intended. The reader may be drawn to Choice B because of the title of the passage and the use of words like "better," but the message of the passage is larger and more general than this.

Passage 2: "When a Poet Longs to Mourn, He Writes an Elegy"

5. C
This question tests the reader's summarization skills. The use of the word "actually" in describing what kind of people poets are, as well as other moments like this, may lead readers to selecting choice B or D, but the author is more information than trying to persuade readers. The author gives no indication that she loves poetry (B) or that people, students specifically (D), should write poems. Choice A is incorrect because the style and content of this paragraph do not match those of a foreword; forewords usually focus on the history or ideas of a specific poem to introduce it more fully and help it stand out against other poems. The author here focuses on several poems and gives broad statements. Instead, she tells a kind

of story about poems, giving three very broad time periods in which to discuss them, thereby giving a brief history of poetry, as choice C states.

6. A
This question tests the reader's summarization skills. Key words in the topic sentences of each of the paragraphs ("oldest," "Renaissance," "modern") should give the reader an idea that the author is moving chronologically. The opening and closing sentence-paragraphs are broad and talk generally. Choice B seems reasonable, but epic poems are mentioned in two paragraphs, eliminating the idea that only new types of poems are used in each paragraph. Choice C is also easily eliminated because the author clearly mentions several different poets, groups of people, and poems. Choice D also seems reasonable, considering that the author does move from older forms of poetry to newer forms, but use of "so (that)" makes this statement false, for the author gives no indication that she is rushing (the paragraphs are about the same size) or that she prefers modern poetry.

7. D
This question tests the reader's attention to detail. The key word is "invented"--it ties together the Mesopotamians, who invented the written word, and the fact that they, as the inventors, also invented and used poetry. The other selections focus on other details mentioned in the passage, such as that the Renaissance's admiration of the Greeks (C) and that Beowulf is in Old English (A). Choice B may seem like an attractive answer because it is unlike the others and because the idea of heroes seems rooted in ancient and early civilizations.

8. B
This question tests the reader's vocabulary and contextualization skills. "Telling" is not an unusual word, but it may be used here in a way that is not familiar to readers, as an adjective rather than a verb in gerund form. Choice A may seem like the obvious answer to a reader looking for a verb to match the use they are familiar with. If the reader understands that the word is being used as an adjective and that choice A is a ploy, they may opt to select choice D, "wordy," but it does not make sense in context. Choice C can be easily eliminated, and doesn't have any connection to the paragraph or passage.

"Significant" (B) does make sense contextually, especially relative to the phrase "give insight" used later in the sentence.

Passage 3: "Winged Victory of Samothrace: the Statue of the Gods"

9. B
This question tests the reader's summarization skills. Choice A is a very broad statement that may or may not be true, and seems to be in context, but has nothing to do with the passage. The author does mention that the statue was probably used on a temple dedicated to the Greek gods (D), but in no way discusses or argues for the gods' attitude toward or claim on these temples or its faucets. Nike does indeed lead the gods into a war (the Titan war), as choice C suggests, but this is not mentioned by the passage and students who know this may be drawn to this answer but have not done a close enough analysis of the text that is actually in the passage. Choice B is appropriately expository, and connects the titular emphasis to the idea that the Greek gods are very important to Greek culture.

10. C
This question tests the reader's summarization skills. The test for question choice C is pulled straight from the paragraph, but is not word-for-word, so it may seem too obvious to be the right answer. The passage does talk about Nike being the goddess of war, as choice A states, but the third paragraph only touches on it and it is an inference that soldiers destroyed the statue, when this question is asking specifically for what the third paragraph actually stated. Choice B is also straight from the text, with a minor but key change: the inclusion of the words "all" and "never" are too limiting and the passage does not suggest that these limits exist. If a reader selects choice D, they are also making an inference that is misguided for this type of question. The paragraph does state that the arms and head are "lost" but does not suggest who lost them.

11. A
This question tests the reader's ability to recognize function in writing. Choice B can be eliminated based on the purpose of the passage, which is expository and not persuasive. The author may or may not feel this way, but the passage does

not show evidence of being argumentative for that purpose. Choices C and D are both details found in the text, but neither of them encompasses the entire message of the passage, which has an overall message of learning about culture from art and making guesses about how the two are related, as suggested by choice A.

12. D
This question tests the reader's ability to understand function within writing. Most of the possible selections are very general statements which may or may not be true. It probably is a student who is taking the test on which this question is featured (A), but the author makes no address to the test taker and is not talking to the audience in terms of the test. Likewise, it may also be true that students read more than adults (C), mandated by schools and grades, but the focus on the verb "read" in the first sentence is too narrow and misses the larger purpose of the passage; the same could be said for selection B. While all the statements could be true, choice D is the most germane, and infers the purpose of the passage without making assumptions that could be incorrect.

Passage 4: "Ways Characters Communicate in Theater"

13. D
This question tests the reader's summarization skills. The question is asking very generally about the message of the passage, and the title, "Ways Characters Communicate in Theater," is one indication of that. The other choices A, B, and C are all directly from the text, and therefore readers may be inclined to select one of them, but are too specific to encapsulate the entirety of the passage and its message.

14. B
The paragraph on soliloquies mentions "To be or not to be," and it is from the context of that paragraph that readers may understand that because "To be or not to be" is a soliloquy, Hamlet will be introspective, or thoughtful, while delivering it. It is true that actors deliver soliloquies alone, and may be "solitary" (A), but "thoughtful" (B) is more true to the overall idea of the paragraph. Readers may choose C because drama and theater can be used interchangeably and the passage mentions that soliloquies are unique to theater (and therefore

drama), but this answer is not specific enough to the paragraph in question. Readers may pick up on the theme of life and death and Hamlet's true intentions and select that he is "hopeless" (D), but those themes are not discussed either by this paragraph or passage, as a close textual reading and analysis confirms.

15. C
This question tests the reader's grammatical skills. Choice B seems logical, but parenthesis are actually considered to be a stronger break in a sentence than commas are, and along this line of thinking, actually disrupt the sentence more. Choices A and D make comparisons between theater and film that are simply not made in the passage, and may or may not be true. This detail does clarify the statement that asides are most unique to theater by adding that it is not completely unique to theater, which may have been why the author didn't chose not to delete it and instead used parentheses to designate the detail's importance (C).

16. C
This question tests the reader's vocabulary and contextualization skills. Choice A may or may not be true, but focuses on the wrong function of the word "give" and ignores the rest of the sentence, which is more relevant to what the passage is discussing. CHoices B and D may also be selected if the reader depends too literally on the word "give," failing to grasp the more abstract function of the word that is the focus of choice C, which also properly acknowledges the entirety of the passage and its meaning.

Passage 5: "Women and Advertising"

17. D
This question tests the reader's summarization skills. The other choices A, B, and C focus on portions of the second paragraph that are too narrow and do not relate to the specific portion of text in question. The complexity of the sentence may mislead students into selecting one of these answers, but rearranging or restating the sentence will lead the reader to the correct answer. In addition, choice A makes an assumption that may or may not be true about the intentions of the company, choice B focuses on one product rather than

the idea of the products, and choice C makes an assumption about women that may or may not be true and is not supported by the text.

18. B
This question tests reader's attention to detail. If a reader selects A, he or she may have picked up on the use of the word "debate" and assumed, very logically, that the two are at odds because they are fighting; however, this is simply not supported in the text. Choice C also uses very specific quotes from the text, but it rearranges them and gives them false meaning. The artists want to elevate their creations above the creations of other artists, thereby showing that they are "creative" and "innovative." Similarly, choice D takes phrases straight from the texts and rearranges and confuses them. The artists are described as wanting to be "creative, innovative, individual people," not the women.

19. A
This question tests reader's vocabulary and summarization skills. This phrase, used by the author, may seem flippant and dismissive if readers focus on the word "whatever" and misinterpret it as a popular, colloquial terms. In this way, the choices B and C may mislead the reader to selecting one of them by including the terms "unimportant" and "stupid," respectively. Choice D is a similar misreading, but doesn't make sense when the phrase is at the beginning of the passage and the entire passage is on media messages. Choice A is literarily and contextually appropriate, and the reader can understand that the author would like to keep the introduction focused on the topic the passage is going to discuss.

20. A
This question tests a reader's inference skills. The extreme use of the word "all" in choice B suggests that every single advertising company are working to be approachable, and while this is not only unlikely, the text specifically states that "more" companies have done this, signifying that they have not all participated, even if it's a possibility that they may some day. The use of the limiting word "only" in choice C lends that answer similar problems; women are still buying from companies who do not care about this message, or those companies would not be in business, and the passage speci-

fies that "many" women are worried about media messages, but not all. Readers may find choice D logical, especially if they are looking to make an inference, and while this may be a possibility, the passage does not suggest or discuss this happening. Choice A is correct based on specifically because of the relation between "still working" in the answer and "will hopefully" and the extensive discussion on companies struggles, which come only with progress, in the text.

Passage 6: "FDR, the Treaty of Versailles, and the Fourteen Points"

21. C
This question tests the reader's summarization skills. The entire passage is leading up to the idea that the president of the US may not have had grounds to assert his Fourteen Points when other countries had lost so much. Choice A is pretty directly inferred by the text, but it does not adequately summarize what the entire passage is trying to communicate. Choice B may also be inferred by the passage when it says that the war is "imminent," but it does not represent the entire message, either. The passage does seem to be in praise of FDR, or at least in respect of him, but it does not in any way claim that he is the smartest president, nor does this represent the many other points included. Choice C is then the obvious answer, and most directly relates to the closing sentences which it rewords.

22. C
This question tests the reader's attention to detail. The passage does state that choices A and B are true, and while those statements are in proximity to the explanation for why the war started, they are not the actual reason given. Choice D is a mix up of words used in the passage, which says that the largest powers were in play but not that this fact somehow started the war. The passage does make a direct statement that a domino effect started the war, supporting choice C as the correct answer.

23. A
This question tests the reader's understanding of functions in writing. Throughout the passage, it states that leaders of other nations were hesitant to accept generous or peaceful terms

because of the grievances of the war, and the great loss of life was chief among these. While the passage does touch on the devastation of deadly weapons (B), the use of this raw, emotional fact serves a much larger purpose, and the focus of the passage is not the weapons. While readers may indeed consider who lost the most soldiers (C) when so many countries were involved and the inequalities of loss are mentioned in the passage, there is no discussion of this in the passage. Choice D is related to A, but choice A is more direct and relates more to the passage.

24. B
This question tests the reader's vocabulary skills. Choice A may seem appealing to readers because it is phonetically similar to "catalyzed," but the two are not related in any other way. Choice C makes sense in context, but if plugged into the sentence creates a redundancy that doesn't make sense. Choice D does also not make sense contextually, even if the reader may consider that funds were needed to create more weaponry, especially if it was advanced.

English Grammar Multiple-Choice

How to Answer English Grammar Multiple-Choice - Verb Tense

This tutorial is designed to help you answer English Grammar multiple-choice questions as well as a very quick refresher on verb tenses. It is assumed that you have some familiarity with the verb tenses covered here. If you find these questions difficulty or do not understand the tense construction, we recommend you seek out additional instruction.

Tenses Covered

1. Past Progressive
2. Present Perfect
3. Present Perfect Progressive
4. Present Progressive
5. Simple Future
6. Simple Future – "Going to" Form
7. Past Perfect Progressive
8. Future Perfect Progressive
9. Future Perfect
10. Future Progressive
11. Past Perfect

1. The Past Progressive Tense

How to Recognize This Tense

He *was running* very fast when he fell.

They *were drinking* coffee when he arrived.

About the Past Progressive Tense

This tense is used to speak of an action that was in progress in the past when another event occurred.

The action was unfolding at a point in the past.

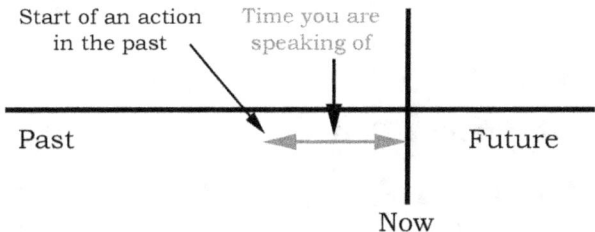

Past Progressive Tense Construction

This tense is formed by using the past tense of the verb "to be" plus the present participle of the main verb.

Sample Question

Bill _____ lunch when we arrived.

    a. will eat
    b. is eating
    c. eats
    d. was eating

How to Answer This Type of Question

1. First examine the question for clues about the time frame.

The sentence ends with "when we arrived," so we know the time frame is a point ("when") in the past (arrived).

The correct answer will refer to an ongoing action at a point of time in the past.

2. Examine the choices and eliminate any obviously incorrect answers.

Choice A is the future tense so we can eliminate.

Choice B is the present continuous so we can eliminate.

Choice C is present tense so we can eliminate.

Choice D refers to an action that takes place at a point of time in the past ("was eating").

2. The Present Perfect Tense

How to Recognize This Tense

I *have had* enough to eat.

We *have been* to Paris many times.

I *have known* him for five years.

I *have been* coming here since I was a child.

About the Present Perfect Tense

This tense expresses the idea that something happened (or didn't happen) at an unspecific time in the past until the present. The action happened at an unspecified time in the past. (If there is a specific time mentioned, the simple past tense is used.) It can be used for repeated action, accomplishments, changes over time and uncompleted action.

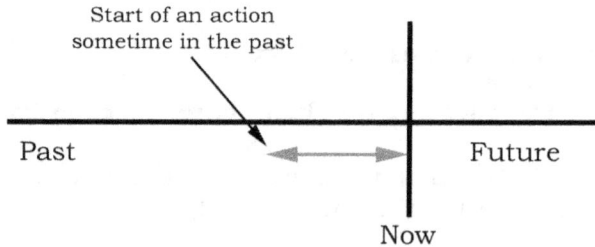

Present Perfect Tense Construction

It is also used with "for" and "since".

This tense is formed by using the present tense of the verb "to have" plus the past participle of the main verb.

Sample Question

I _____ these birds many times.

    a. am seeing
    b. will saw
    c. have seen
    d. have saw

How to Answer This Type of Question

1. First examine the question for clues about the time frame.

"Many times" tells us that the action is repeated and in the past.

2. Examine the choices and eliminate any obviously incorrect answers.

Choice A, "am seeing" is incorrect because it is a continuing action, i.e. in the present; it also doesn't use a form of 'have'.

Choice B is grammatically incorrect.

Choice C tells of something that has happened in the past and is now over. Best choice so far.

Choice D is grammatically incorrect.

3. The Present Perfect Progressive Tense

How to Recognize This Tense

We *have been seeing* a lot of rainy days.

I *have been reading* some very good books.

About the Present Perfect Progressive Tense

This tense expresses the idea that something happened (or didn't happen) in the relatively recent past, but <u>the action is not finished.</u> It is used to express the duration of the action.

NOTE: The present perfect speaks of an action that happened sometime in the past, but this action is finished. In the present perfect progressive tense, the action that started in the past is still going on.

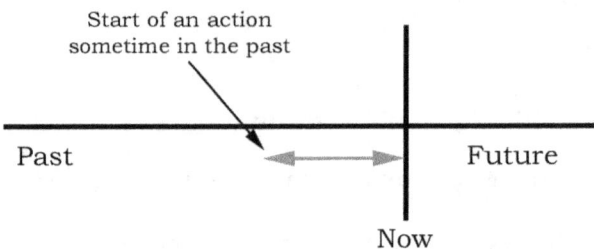

Present Perfect Progressive Tense Construction

This tense is formed by using the present tense of the verb "to have," plus "been," plus the present participle of the main verb.

Sample Question

Bill _____ there for two hours.

    a. sits
    b. sitting
    c. has been sitting
    d. will sat

How to Answer This Type of Question

1. First examine the question for clues about the time frame.

"For two hours" tells us that the action, "sits," is continuous up to now, and may continue into the future.

Note this sentence could also be the simple past tense,

Bill sat there for two hours.

Or the future tense,

Bill will sit there for two hours.

However, these are not among the options.

2. Examine the choices and eliminate any obviously incorrect answers.

Choice A is incorrect because it is the present tense.
Choice B is incorrect because it is the present continuous.
Choice C is correct. "Has been sitting" expresses a continuous action in the past that isn't finished.
Choice D is grammatically incorrect.

4. The Present Progressive Tense

How to Recognize This Tense

We *are having* a delicious lunch.

They *are driving* much too fast.

About the Present Progressive Tense

This tense is used to express what the action is <u>right now</u>. The action started in the recent past, and is continuing into the future.

Present Perfect Tense Construction

The Present Progressive Tense is formed by using the present tense of "to be" plus the present participle of the main verb.

Sample Question

She _____ very hard these days.

    a. works
    b. is working
    c. will work
    d. worked

How to Answer This Type of Question

1. First examine the question for clues about the time frame.

The end of the sentence includes "these days" which tell us the action started in the past, continues into the present, and may continue into the future.

2. Examine the choices and eliminate any obviously incorrect answers.

Choice A, the simple present is incorrect.
Choice B, "is working" is correct.
Check the other two choices just to be sure. Choice C is future tense, and choice D is past tense, so they can be eliminated.
The correct answer is choice B.

5. The Simple Future Tense

How to Recognize This Tense

I *will see* you tomorrow.
We *will drive* the car.

About the Simple Future Tense

This tense shows that the action will happen some time in the future.

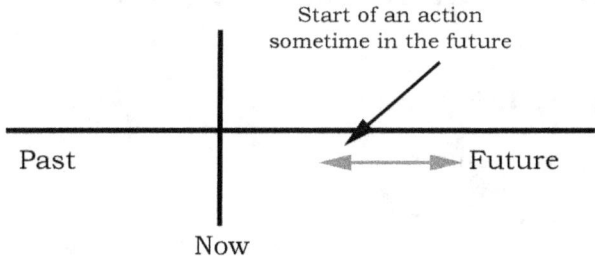

Simple Future Tense Construction

The tense is formed by using "will" plus the root form of the verb. (The root form of the verb is the infinitive without "to." Examples: read, swim.)

Sample Question

We _____ to Paris next year.

    a. went
    b. had been
    c. will go
    d. go

How to Answer This Type of Question

1. First examine the question for clues about the time frame.

The last two words of the sentence, "next year," clearly identify this sentence as referring to the future.

2. Examine the choices and eliminate any obviously incorrect answers.
Choice A is the past tense and can be eliminated.

Choice B is the past perfect tense and can be eliminated.

Choice D is the simple present and can be eliminated.

Choice C is the only one left and is the correct simple future tense.

6. The Simple Future Tense – The "Going to" Form

How to Recognize This Tense

I *am going to* see you tomorrow.

We *are going to* drive the car.

About the Simple Future Tense

This form of the future tense is used to show the intention of doing something in the future. (This is the strict grammatical meaning, but in daily speech, it is often used interchangeably with the simple future tense, the "will" form.)

The tense is formed by using the present conditional tense of "to go," plus the infinitive of the verb.

Sample Question

I _____ shopping in an hour.

    a. go
    b. have gone
    c. am going to go
    d. went

How to Answer This Type of Question

1. First examine the question for clues about the time frame.

"In an hour" clearly identifies the action as taking place in the future.

2. Examine the choices and eliminate any obviously incorrect answers.

Choice A is the simple present tense and can be eliminated.

Choice B is the past perfect and can be eliminated.

Choice C is the correct answer.

Choice D is the past tense and can be eliminated.

7. The Past Perfect Progressive Tense

How to Recognize This Tense

I *had been sleeping* for an hour when you phoned.

We *had been eating* our dinner when they all came into the dining room.

About the Past Perfect Progressive Tense

This tense is used to show that the action had been going on for a period of time in the past when another action, also in the past, occurred.

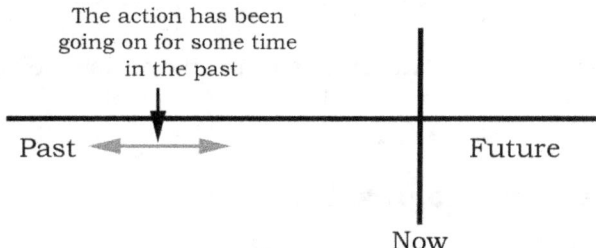

Past Perfect Tense Construction

The tense is formed by using the past perfect tense of the verb "to be" plus the present participle of the main verb.

Sample Question

How long _____ you _____ when I saw you?

    a. are ____ running
    b. had ____ running
    c. had ____ been running
    d. was ____ running

How to Answer This Type of Question

1. First examine the question for clues about the time frame.

"When I saw" tells us the sentence happened at a point of time ("when") in the past ("saw").

2. Examine the choices and eliminate any obviously incorrect answers.

Choice A, "are running" is incorrect and can be eliminated.

Choice B, "Had ___ running" is grammatically incorrect and can be eliminated.

Choice C is correct.

Choice D is grammatically incorrect so the answer is Choice C.

8. Future Perfect Progressive Tense

How to Recognize This Tense

I *will have been working* here for two years in March.

I *will have been driving* for four hours when I get there, so I will be tired.

About the Future Perfect Progressive Tense

This tense is used to show that the action continues up to a point of time in the future.

Future Prefect Progressive Tense Construction

This tense is formed by using the future perfect tense of "to be" plus the present participle of the main verb.

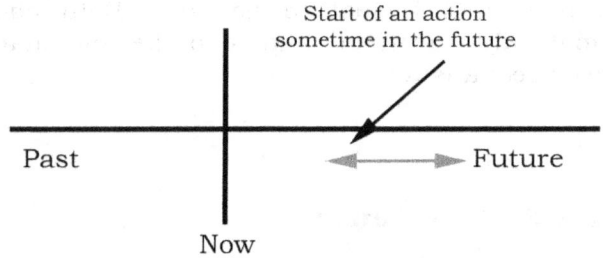

Sample Question

_____ you _____ all the time I am gone?

      a. have _____ been working
      b. will _____ have been working
      c. are _____ worked
      d. will _____ worked

How to Answer This Type of Question

1. First examine the question for clues about the time frame.

"All the time I am gone" refers to an action in the future ("time I am gone") and the action is progressive ("all the time"). The progressive action means the correct choice will be a verb tense that ends in "ing."

2. Examine the choices and eliminate any obviously incorrect answers.

Choice A, the past perfect, refers to a past continuous event and is also grammatically incorrect in the sentence, so choice A can be eliminated.

Choice B looks correct because it refers to an action will be going on for a period of time in the future.

Examine choices C and D just to be sure. Both choices are grammatically incorrect and can be eliminated. Choice B is the correct answer.

9. The Future Perfect Tense

How to Recognize This Tense

By next November, I *will have received* my promotion.

By the time he gets home, she is going *to have cleaned* the entire house.

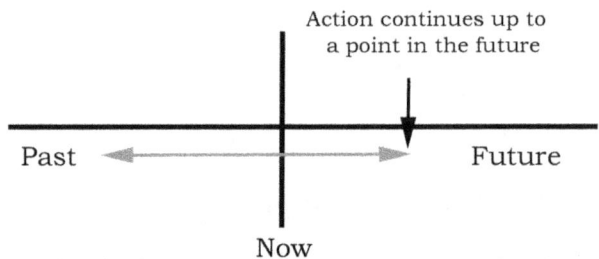

About the Future Perfect Tense

The future perfect tense expresses action in the future before another action in the future. This is the past in the future. For example:

He *will have prepared* dinner when she arrives.

Future Perfect Tense Construction

This tense is formed by "will + have + past participle."

Sample Question

They _____ their seats before the game begins.

    a. will have find
    b. will find
    c. will have found
    d. found

How to Answer This Type of Question

1. First examine the question for clues about the time frame.

This question could be several different tenses. The only clue about the time frame is "before the game begins," which refers to a specific point of time.

We know it isn't in the past, because "begins" is incorrect for the past tense. Similarly with the present. So the question is about something that happens in the future, before another event in the future.

2. Examine the choices and eliminate any obviously incorrect answers.

Choice A can be eliminated as incorrect.
Choice B looks good, so mark it and check the others before making a final decision.
Choice C is the past perfect and can be eliminated because the time frame is incorrect.
Choice D is the simple past tense and can be eliminated for the same reason.

10. Future Progressive Tense

How to Recognize This Tense

The teams *will be playing* soccer when we arrive.

At 3:45 the soccer fans *will be waiting* for the game to start at 4:00 o'clock

At 3:45 the soccer players *will be preparing* to play at 4:00 o'clock

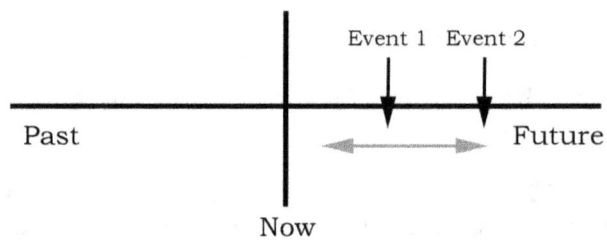

About the Future Progressive Tense

The future progressive tense talks about a continuing action in the future.

Future Progressive Tense Construction

will+ be + (root form) + ing = will be playing

Sample Question

Many excited fans _____ a bus to see the game at 4:00.

    a. catch
    b. catching
    c. have been catching
    d. will be catching

How to Answer This Type of Question

1. First examine the question for clues about the time frame.

"At 4:00," tells us the sentence is either in the past OR in the future.

2. Examine the choices and eliminate any obviously incorrect answers.

From the time frame of the sentence, the answer will be past or future tense.

Choice A is the present tense and can be eliminated.
Choice B is the present continuous tense and can be eliminated.
Choice C is the past perfect continuous and can be eliminated.
Choice D is the only one left. Quickly examining the tense, it is future progressive and is correct in the sentence.

11. The Past Perfect Tense

How to Recognize This Tense

The party *had* just *started* when the coach arrived.

We *had waited* for twenty minutes when the bus finally came.

About the Past Perfect

The past perfect tense talks about two events that happened in the past and establishes which event happened first.

Another example is, "We had eaten when he arrived."

The two events are "eat" and "he arrived." From the sentence above the past perfect tense tells us the first event, "eat" happened before the second event, "he arrived."

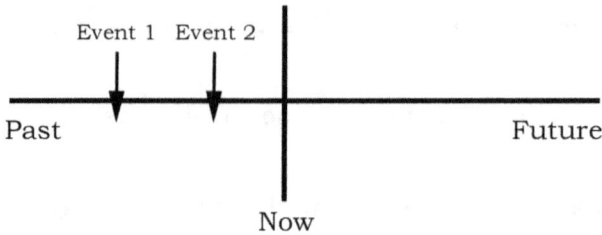

I had already eaten when my friends arrived.

Past Perfect Tense Construction

The past perfect is formed by "have" plus the past participle.

Sample Question

It was time to go home after they _____ the game.

    a. will win

    b. win

    c. had won

    d. wins

How to Answer This Type of Question

1. First examine the question for clues about the time frame.

"Was" tells us the sentence happened in the past. Also notice there are two events, "go home" and "after the game."

2. Examine the choices and eliminate any obviously incorrect answers.

Choice A is the future tense and can be eliminated. Choice B is the simple present and can be eliminated. Choice C is the past perfect and orders the two events in the past. Choice D is the present tense and incorrect and can be eliminated, so choice C is the correct answer.

Common English Usage Mistakes - A Quick Review

Like some parts of English grammar, usage is definitely going to be on the exam and there isn't any tricky strategies or shortcuts to help you get through this section.
Here is a quick review of common usage mistakes.

1. May and Might

'May' can act as a principle verb, which can express permission or possibility.
Examples:

Lets wait, the meeting may have started.
May I begin now?

'May' can act as an auxiliary verb, which an expresses a purpose or wish

Examples:

May you find favour in the sight of your employer.

May your wishes come true.
People go to school so that they may be educated.

The past tense of may is might.

Examples:

I asked if I might begin

'Might' can be used to signify a weak or slim possibility or polite suggestion.

Examples:

You might find him in his office, but I doubt it.
You might offer to help if you want to.

2. Lie and Lay

The verb lay should always take an object. The three forms of the verb lay are: laid, lay and laid.

The verb lie (recline) should not take any object. The three forms of the verb lie are: lay, lie and lain.

Examples:

Lay on the bed.
The tables were laid by the students.
Let the little kid lie.
The patient lay on the table.

The dog has lain there for 30 minutes.

Note: The verb lie can also mean "to tell a falsehood". This verb can appear in three forms: lied, lie, and lied. This is different from the verb lie (recline) mentioned above.

Examples:

The accused is fond of telling lies.
Did she lie?

3. Would and should

The past tense of shall is 'should', and so "should" generally follows the same principles as "shall."

The past tense of will is "would," and so "would" generally follows the same principles as "will."

The two verbs 'would and should' can be correctly used interchangeably to signify obligation. The two verbs also have some unique uses too. Should is used in three persons to signify obligation.

Examples:

I should go after work.

People should do exercises everyday.
You should be generous.

"Would" is specially used in any of the three persons, to signify willingness, determination and habitual action.

Examples:

They would go for a test run every Saturday.
They would not ignore their duties.
She would try to be punctual.

4. Principle and Auxiliary Verbs

Two principle verbs can be used along with one auxiliary verb as long as the auxiliary verb form suits the two principle verbs.

Examples:

A number of people have been employed and some promoted.

A new tree has been planted and the old has been cut down.

Again note the difference in the verb form.

5. Can and Could

A. Can is used to express capacity or ability.

Examples:

I can complete the assignment today
He can meet up with his target.

B. Can is also used to express permission.

Examples:

Yes, you can begin

In the sentence below, "can" was used to mean the same thing as "may." However, the difference is that the word "can" is used for negative or interrogative sentences, while "may" is used in affirmative sentences to express possibility.

Examples:

They may be correct.   Positive sentence - use may.
Can this statement be correct? A question using "can."
It cannot be correct. Negative sentence using "can."

The past tense of can is could. It can serve as a principle verb when it is used to express its own meaning.

Examples:

In spite of the difficulty of the test, he could still perform well. "Could" here is used to express ability.

6. Ought

The verb ought should normally be followed by the word to.

Examples:

I *ought to* close shop now.

The verb 'ought' can be used to express:

A. Desirability

You ought to wash your hands before eating. It is desirable to wash your hands.

B. Probability

She ought to be on her way back by now. She is probably on her way.

C. Moral obligation or duty

The government ought to protect the oppressed. It is the government's duty to protect the oppressed.

7. Raise and Rise

Rise
The verb rise means to go up, or to ascend.
The verb rise can appear in three forms, rose, rise, and risen.
The verb should not take an object.

Examples:

The bird rose very slowly.
The trees rise above the house.
My aunt has risen in her career.

Raise
The verb raise means to increase, to lift up.
The verb raise can appear in three forms, raised, raise and raised.

Examples:

He raised his hand.
The workers requested a raise.
Do not raise that subject.

8. Past Tense and Past Participle

Pay attention to the proper use these verbs: sing, show, ring, awake, fly, flow, begin, hang and sink.

Mistakes usually occur when using the past participle and past tense of these verbs as they are often mixed up.

Each of these verbs can appear in three forms:

Sing, Sang, Sung.
Show, Showed, Showed/Shown.
Ring, Rang, Rung.
Awake, awoke, awaken
Fly, Flew, Flown.
Flow, Flowed, Flowed.
Begin, Began, Begun.
Hang, Hanged, Hanged (a criminal)

Hang, Hung, Hung (a picture)
Sink, Sank, Sunk.

Examples:

The stranger rang the door bell. (simple past tense)
I have rung the door bell already. (past participle - an action completed in the past)

The stone sank in the river. (simple past tense)
The stone had already sunk. (past participle - an action completed in the past)

The meeting began at 4:00.
The meeting has begun.

9. Shall and Will

When speaking informally, the two can be used interchangeably. In formal writing, they must be used correctly.

"Will" is used in the second or third person, while "shall" is used in the first person. Both verbs are used to express a time or even in the future.

Examples:

I shall, We shall (First Person)
You will (Second Person)
They will (Third Person)

This principle however reverses when the verbs are to be used to express threats, determination, command, willingness, promise or compulsion. In these instances, will is now used in first person and shall in the second and third person.

Examples:

I will be there next week, no matter what.
This is a promise, so the first person "I" takes "will."
You shall ensure that the work is completed.
This is a command, so the second person "you" takes "shall."

I will try to make payments as promised.
This is a promise, so the first person "I" takes "will."

They shall have arrived by the end of the day.
This is a determination, so the third person "they" takes shall.

Note
A. The two verbs, shall and will should not occur twice in the same sentence when the same future is being referred to

Example:

I shall arrive early if my driver is here on time.

B. Will should not be used in the first person when questions are being asked

Examples:

Shall I go ?
Shall we go?

Subject Verb Agreement

Verbs in any sentence must agree with the subject of the sentence both in person and number. Problems usually occur when the verb doesn't correspond with the right subject or the verb fails to match the noun close to it.

Unfortunately, there is no easy way around these principles - no tricky strategy or easy rule. You just have to memorize them.

Here is a quick review:

The verb to be, present (past)

Person	Singular	Plural
First	I am (was)	we are (were)
Second	you are (were)	you are (were)
Third	he, she, it is (was)	they are (were)

The verb to have, present (past)

Person	Singular	Plural
First	I have (had)	we have (had)
Second	you have (had)	you have (had)
Third	he, she, it has (had)	they have (had)

Regular verbs, e.g. to walk, present (past)

Person	Singular	Plural
First	I walk (walked)	we walk (walked)
Second	you walk (walked)	you walk (walked)
Third	he, she, it walks (walked)	they work (walked)

1. Every and Each

When nouns are qualified by "every" or "each," they take a singular verb even if they are joined by 'and'

Examples:

Each mother and daughter *was* a given separate test.
Every teacher and student *was* properly welcomed.

2. Plural Nouns

Nouns like measles, tongs, trousers, riches, scissors etc. are all plural.

Examples:

The trousers *are* dirty.
My scissors *have* gone missing.
The tongs *are* on the table.

3. With and As Well

Two subjects linked with "with" or "as well" should have a verb that matches the first subject.

Examples:

The pencil, with the papers and equipment, *is* on the desk.
David as well as Louis is coming.

4. Plural Nouns

The following nouns take a singular verb:

> politics, mathematics, innings, news, advice, summons, furniture, information, poetry, machinery, vacation, scenery

Examples:

The machinery *is* difficult to assemble
The furniture *has* been delivered
The scenery *was* beautiful

5. Single Entities

A proper noun in plural form that refers to a single entity requires a singular verb. This is a complicated way of saying; some things appear to be plural, but are really singular, or some nouns refer to a collection of things but the collection is really singular.

Examples:

The United Nations Organization *is* the decision maker in the matter.

Here the "United Nations Organization" is really only one "thing" or noun, but is made up of many "nations."

The book, "The Seven Virgins" *was* not available in the library.

Here there is only one book, although the title of the book is plural.

6. Specific Amounts are always singular

A plural noun that refers to a specific amount or quantity that is considered as a whole (dozen, hundred, score etc) requires a singular verb.

Examples:

60 minutes *is* quite a long time.
Here "60 minutes" is considered a whole, and therefore one item (singular noun).

The first million is the most difficult.

7. Either, Neither and Each are always singular

The verb is always singular when used with: either, each, neither, every one and many.

Examples:

Either of the boys *is* lying.
Each of the employees *has* been well compensated
Many a police officer *has* been found to be courageous
Every one of the teachers *is* responsible

8. Linking with Either, Or, and Neither match the second subject

Two subjects linked by "either," "or,""nor" or "neither" should have a verb that matches the second subject.

Examples:

Neither David nor Paul *will* be coming.
Either Mary or Tina *is* paying.

Note
If one of the subjects linked by "either," "or,""nor" or "neither" is in plural form, then the verb should also be in plural, and the verb should be close to the plural subject.

Examples:
Neither the mother *nor* her kids *have* eaten.
Either Mary *or* her *friends are* paying.

9. Collective Nouns are Plural

Some collective nouns such as poultry, gentry, cattle, vermin etc. are considered plural and require a plural verb.

Examples:

The *poultry are* sick.
The *cattle are* well fed.

Note
Collective nouns involving people can work with both plural and singular verbs.

Examples:

Nigerians are known to be hard working
Europeans live in Africa

10. Nouns that are Singular and Plural

Nouns like deer, sheep, swine, salmon etc. can be singular or plural and require the same verb form.

Examples:

The swine is feeding. (singular)
The swine are feeding. (plural)

The salmon is on the table. (singular)
The salmon are running upstream. (plural)

11. Collective Nouns are Singular

Collective nouns such as Army, Jury, Assembly, Committee, Team etc should carry a singular verb when they subscribe to one idea. If the ideas or views are more than one, then the verb used should be plural.

Examples:

The committee is in agreement in their decision.

The committee were in disagreement in their decision.
The jury has agreed on a verdict.

The jury were unable to agree on a verdict.

12. Subjects links by "and" are plural.

Two subjects linked by "and" always require a plural verb

Examples:

David and John are students.

Note
If the subjects linked by "and" are used as one phrase, or constitute one idea, then the verb must be singular

The color of his socks and shoe is black.
Here "socks and shoe" are two nouns, however the subject is "color" which is singular.

English Grammar and Usage Answer Sheet

	A	B	C	D	E		A	B	C	D	E
1	○	○	○	○	○	31	○	○	○	○	○
2	○	○	○	○	○	32	○	○	○	○	○
3	○	○	○	○	○	33	○	○	○	○	○
4	○	○	○	○	○	34	○	○	○	○	○
5	○	○	○	○	○	35	○	○	○	○	○
6	○	○	○	○	○	36	○	○	○	○	○
7	○	○	○	○	○	37	○	○	○	○	○
8	○	○	○	○	○	38	○	○	○	○	○
9	○	○	○	○	○	39	○	○	○	○	○
10	○	○	○	○	○	40	○	○	○	○	○
11	○	○	○	○	○	41	○	○	○	○	○
12	○	○	○	○	○	42	○	○	○	○	○
13	○	○	○	○	○	43	○	○	○	○	○
14	○	○	○	○	○	44	○	○	○	○	○
15	○	○	○	○	○	45	○	○	○	○	○
16	○	○	○	○	○	46	○	○	○	○	○
17	○	○	○	○	○	47	○	○	○	○	○
18	○	○	○	○	○	48	○	○	○	○	○
19	○	○	○	○	○	49	○	○	○	○	○
20	○	○	○	○	○	50	○	○	○	○	○
21	○	○	○	○	○	51	○	○	○	○	○
22	○	○	○	○	○	52	○	○	○	○	○
23	○	○	○	○	○	53	○	○	○	○	○
24	○	○	○	○	○	54	○	○	○	○	○
25	○	○	○	○	○	55	○	○	○	○	○
26	○	○	○	○	○	56	○	○	○	○	○
27	○	○	○	○	○	57	○	○	○	○	○
28	○	○	○	○	○	58	○	○	○	○	○
29	○	○	○	○	○	59	○	○	○	○	○
30	○	○	○	○	○	60	○	○	○	○	○

English Grammar Practice Questions

1. **Choose the sentence with the correct grammar.**

   a. The man was asked to come with his daughter and her test results.

   b. The man was asked to come with her daughter and her test results.

   c. The man was asked to come with her daughter and our test results.

   d. None of the above.

2. **Choose the sentence with the correct grammar.**

   a. Every doctor must come with his stethoscope

   b. Every doctor must come with their stethoscope

   c. Every doctor must come with our stethoscope

   d. None of the above.

3. **Choose the sentence with the correct grammar.**

   a. Each of them have to be given a ticket.

   b. Each of them is to be given a ticket.

   c. Each of them are to be given a ticket.

   d. None of the above.

4. **Choose the sentence with the correct grammar.**

   a. The scenery were breathtaking.

   b. The scenery was breathtaking.

   c. Both of the above

   d. None of the above

5. Choose the sentence with the correct grammar.

    a. Neither the teacher nor the student is left in class.
    b. Neither the teacher nor the student are left in class.
    c. Both of the above.
    d. None of the above.

6. Choose the sentence with the proper usage.

    a. The meeting may have started.
    b. The meeting might have started.
    c. Both of the above.
    d. None of the above.

7. Choose the sentence with the proper usage.

    a. He can be correct
    b. He could be correct
    c. He may be correct
    d. None of the above

8. Choose the sentence with the correct grammar.

    a. The vermin are to be exterminated.
    b. The vermin is to be exterminated.
    c. The vermin was to be exterminated.
    d. None of the above.

9. Choose the sentence with the correct grammar.

    a. The salmon has been cooked.
    b. The salmon have been cooked.
    c. Both of the above.
    d. None of the above.

10. Choose the sentence with the correct grammar.

a. Many of the students came with their lunch box.
b. Many of the students came with our lunch box.
c. Many of the students came with his or her lunch box.
d. None of the above.

11. Choose the sentence with the correct grammar.

a. The driver and the cleaner were to be sacked.
b. The driver and the cleaner are to be sacked.
c. The driver and the cleaner is to be sacked.
d. None of the above.

12. Choose the sentence with the correct grammar.

a. Here are the names of people whom you should contact.
b. Here are the names of people who you should contact.
c. Both of the above.
d. None of the above.

13. Choose the sentence with the proper usage.

a. Christians believe that their lord have raised.
b. Christians believe that their lord have risen.
c. Christians believe that their lord have raise.
d. None of the above.

14. Choose the sentence with the proper usage.

a. I will be at the office by 9 a. m.
b. I shall be at the office by 9 a. m.
c. Both of the above.
d. None of the above.

15. Choose the sentence with the correct grammar.

    a. The army are interested in buying the property.
    b. The army is interested in buying the property.
    c. The army were interested in buying the property.
    d. None of the above.

16. Choose the sentence with the correct grammar.

    a. The poultry is sold off yesterday.
    b. The poultry were sold off yesterday.
    c. The poultry was sold off yesterday.
    d. None of the above.

17. Choose the sentence with the correct grammar.

    a. Mark and Peter have stopped to each other.
    b. Mark and Peter have stopped to one another.
    c. Both of the above.
    d. None of the above.

18. Choose the sentence with the correct grammar.

    a. The teacher asked everybody is to submit his assignment by 9 a.m.
    b. The teacher asked everybody is to submit our assignment by 9 a.m.
    c. The teacher asked everybody is to submit their assignment by 9 a.m.
    d. None of the above.

19. Choose the sentence with the proper usage.

    a. I will ensure that you receive the proper reward.
    b. I shall ensure that you receive the proper reward.
    c. Both of the above.
    d. None of the above.

20. Choose the sentence with the proper usage.

   a. He ought to be back by now.
   b. He ought be back by now.
   c. He ought come back by now.
   d. None of the above.

21. Choose the sentence with the correct grammar.

   a. The gentry were well taken off at the reception.
   b. The gentry was well taken off at the reception.
   c. The gentry are well taken off at the reception.
   d. None of the above.

22. Choose the sentence with the correct grammar.

   a. The deer are running for their lives.
   b. The deer is running for their lives.
   c. Both of the above.
   d. None of the above.

23. Choose the sentence with the correct grammar.

   a. His measles is getting better.
   b. His measles are getting better.
   c. Both of the above.
   d. None of the above.

24. Choose the sentence with the correct grammar.

   a. Each player gets a locker to keep their personal things.
   b. Each player gets a locker to keep his personal things.
   c. Each player gets a locker to keep our personal things.
   d. None of the above.

25. Choose the sentence with the proper usage.

    a. The tables were laid by the students.
    b. The tables were lay by the students.
    c. The tables were lie by the students.
    d. None of the above.

26. Choose the sentence with the correct grammar.

    a. The teachers and the student are standing in the hall.
    b. The teachers and the student is standing in the hall.
    c. Both of the above.
    d. None of the above.

27. Choose the sentence with the proper usage.

    a. Shall I give my speech now?
    b. Will I give my speech now?
    c. Both of the above.
    d. None of the above.

28. Choose the sentence with the correct grammar.

    a. Any girl that fails the test loses their admission.
    b. Any girl that fails the test loses our admission.
    c. Any girl that fails the test loses her admission.
    d. None of the above.

29. Choose the sentence with the proper usage.

    a. The dog has lay there for 30 minutes.
    b. The dog has lie there for 30 minutes.
    c. The dog has lain there for 30 minutes.
    d. None of the above.

30. Choose the sentence with the correct grammar.

    a. The sad news were delivered this morning.
    b. The sad news are delivered this morning.
    c. The sad news was delivered this morning.
    d. None of that above.

31. Choose the sentence with the proper usage.

    a. He told him to raised it up.
    b. He told him to raise it up.
    c. He told him to rise it up.
    d. None of the above.

32. Choose the sentence with the correct grammar.

    a. Neither of them came with their bicycle.
    b. Neither of them came with his bicycle.
    c. Neither of them came with our bicycle.
    d. None of the above.

33. Choose the sentence with the proper usage.

    a. A number of people have been employed and others promoted.
    b. A number of people have been sacked and others have been employed.
    c. A number of people sacked and others have been promoted.
    d. None of the above.

34. Choose the sentence with the correct grammar.

a. Politics were a dirty game.

b. Politics is a dirty game.

c. Politics are a dirty game.

d. None of the above.

35. Choose the sentence with the correct grammar.

a. The members of the team were asked to discuss with each other.

b. The members of the team were asked to discuss with one another.

c. Both of the above.

d. None of the above.

36. Choose the sentence with the correct grammar.

a. Their wages is been cut by half.

b. Their wages has been cut by half.

c. Their wages have been cut by half.

d. None of the above.

37. Choose the sentence with the proper usage.

a. In spite of the BAD weather yesterday, he can still attend the party.

b. In spite of the BAD weather yesterday, he could still attend the party.

c. In spite of the BAD weather yesterday, he may still attend the party.

d. None of the above.

38. Choose the sentence with the correct grammar.

a. The World Health Organization (WHO) were meeting by January.

b. The World Health Organization (WHO) are meeting by January.

c. The World Health Organization (WHO) is meeting by January.

d. None of the above.

39. Choose the sentence with the correct grammar.

a. Everyone was asked to raise their hand.

b. Everyone was asked to raise our hand.

c. Everyone was asked to raise her hand.

d. None of the above.

40. Choose the sentence with the proper usage.

a. They never and never will disobey the rules.

b. They never have and never will disobey the rules.

c. Both of the above.

d. None of the above.

41. Choose the sentence with the correct grammar.

a. Neither of them were coming along.

b. Neither of them is coming along.

c. Neither of them are coming along.

d. None of the above.

42. Choose the sentence with the correct grammar.

a. Everyone are to wear a black tie.

b. Everyone have to wear a black tie.

c. Everyone has to wear a black tie.

d. None of the above.

43. Choose the sentence with the proper usage.

  a. She was nodding her head, her hips are swaying.
  b. She was nodding her head, her hips is swaying.
  c. She was nodding her head, her hips were swaying.
  d. None of the above

44. Choose the sentence with the correct grammar.

  a. The broken furniture has been replaced.
  b. The broken furniture have been replaced.
  c. The broken furniture is been replaced.
  d. None of the above.

45. Choose the sentence with the correct grammar.

  a. Who would be giving the opening address?
  b. Whom will be giving the opening address?
  c. Both of the above.
  d. None of the above.

46. Choose the sentence with the correct grammar.

  a. 15 minutes is all the time you have to complete the test.
  b. 15 minutes are all the time you have to complete the test.
  c. Both of the above.
  d. None of the above.

47. Choose the sentence with the proper usage.

  a. They will have to retire when they reach 60 years of age.
  b. They shall have to retire when they reach 60 years of age.
  c. Both of the above.
  d. None of the above.

48. Choose the sentence with the correct grammar.

    a. The scissors are on the table
    b. The scissors is on the table
    c. Both of the above
    d. None of the above

49. Choose the sentence with the correct grammar.

    a. The new machinery were working at full capacity
    b. The new machinery are working at full capacity
    c. The new machinery is working at full capacity
    c. None of the above

50. Choose the sentence with the correct grammar.

    a. Either Paul or Mary is the thief
    b. Either Paul or Mary are the thief
    c. Either Paul or Mary were the thief
    d. None of the above

Answer Key

1. A
A pronoun should conform to its antecedent in gender, number and person.

2. A
Words such as neither, each, many, either, every, everyone, everybody and any should take a singular pronoun.

3. B
Use a singular verb with either, each, neither, everyone and many.

4. B
Always use the singular verb form for nouns like politics, wages, mathematics, innings, news, advice, summons, furniture, information, poetry, machinery, vacation, scenery etc.

5. A
When two subjects are linked by "either," "or," "nor," or "neither," use a verb that matches the second subject.

6. A
The verb "may" is used to express possibility or permission. Might is the past tense of may. In casual conversation, may and might are often used interchangeably, however, although it is grammatically incorrect.

7. C
Although the CAN could be used to mean the same thing as the word MAY, the difference is that the word can is used for negative or interrogative sentences, while may is used in affirmative sentences to express possibility.

8. A
Use the plural verb form with collective nouns such as poultry, gentry, cattle, vermin etc.

9. C
Nouns like deer, sheep, swine, salmon etc can take a singular or plural verb depending if they are used in their singular or

plural form.

10. C
Words such as neither, each, many, either, every, everyone, everybody and any should take a singular pronoun.

11. B
Two subjects linked by "and" with the use of the article "the" affects the nature of the verb to be used and so a plural verb is required.

12. A
Use "whom" in the objective case, and use "who" a subjective case.

13. B
The verb rise ('to go up', 'to ascend.') can appear in three forms, rise, rose, and risen. The verb should not take an object.

14. B
"Will" is used in the second or third person (they, he, she and you), while "shall" is used in the first person (I and we). Both verbs are used to express futurity. In common usage and everyday conversation, however, they can be interchanged.

15. B
Use the singular verb form with collective nouns such as army, jury, assembly, committee, team etc. when they subscribe to one idea. If the ideas or views are more than one, use the plural form.

16. B
Use the plural verb form with collective nouns such as poultry, gentry, cattle, vermin etc.

17. A
When you use 'each other' it should be used for two things or people. When you use 'one another' it should be used for things and people above two

18. A
Words such as neither, each, many, either, every, everyone, everybody and any should take a singular pronoun.

19. B
"Shall" is used in the second or third person (they, he, she and you), while "will" is used in the first person (I and we) when they are used to express threats, determination, command, willingness, promise or compulsion.

20. A
The verb "ought" can be used to express desirability, duty and probability. The verb is usually followed by "to."

21. A
Use the plural verb form with collective nouns such as poultry, gentry, cattle, vermin etc.

22. A
Nouns like deer, sheep, swine, salmon etc can take a singular or plural verb depending if they are used in their singular or plural form.

23. B
Use a plural verb for nouns like measles, tongs, trousers, riches, scissors etc.

24. B
Words such as neither, each, many, either, every, everyone, everybody and any should take a singular pronoun.

25. A
The verb LAY should always take an object. Here the subject is the table. The three forms of the verb lay are: lay, laid and laid. The sentence above is in past tense.

26. A
When two subjects are linked with "with" or "as well," use the verb form that matches the first subject.

27. A
"Will" is used in the second or third person (they, he, she and you), while "shall" is used in the first person (I and we) when questions are asked.

28. C
Words such as neither, each, many, either, every, everyone, everybody and any should take a singular pronoun.

29. C
The verb lie (recline) should not take an object. The three forms of the verb lie are: l lie, lay and lain. The sentence above is in past tense.

30. C
Always use the singular verb form for nouns like politics, wages, mathematics, innings, news, advice, summons, furniture, information, poetry, machinery, vacation, scenery etc.

31. B
The verb raise ('to increase', 'to lift up.') can appear in three forms, raise, raised and raised.

32. B
Use a singular pronoun with words such as neither, each, many, either, every, everyone, everybody and any. Here we are assuming that the subject is male, and so use "his." The subject could be female, in which case we would use "her," however that is not a choice here.

33. B
Two principal verbs can be used along with one auxiliary verb as long as the auxiliary verb form suits the two principal verbs.

34. B
Always use the singular verb form for nouns like politics, wages, mathematics, innings, news, advice, summons, furniture, information, poetry, machinery, vacation, scenery etc.

35. B
When you use 'each other' it should be used for two things or people. When you use 'one another' it should be used for things and people above two.

36. C
Always use the singular verb form for nouns like politics, wages, mathematics, innings, news, advice, summons, furniture, information, poetry, machinery, vacation, scenery etc.

37. B
Use "could," the past tense of "can" to express ability or capacity.

38. C
Use a singular verb with a proper noun in plural form that refers to a single entity. Here the "The World Health Organization" is a single entity, although it is made up on many members.

39. C
Words such as neither, each, many, either, every, everyone, everybody and any should take a singular pronoun. Here we are assuming that the subject is female, and so use "her." The subject could be male, in which case we would use "his," however that is not one of the choices in this case.

40. B
One principal verb can be used correctly with two auxiliary verbs as long as the form of principal verb used suits the two auxiliary verbs.

41. B
Use a singular verb with either, each, neither, everyone and many.

42. C
Use a singular verb with either, each, neither, everyone and many.

43. C
A verb can fit any of the two subjects in a compound sentence as long as the verb form agrees with that subject.

44. A
Always use the singular verb form for nouns like politics, wages, mathematics, innings, news, advice, summons,

furniture, information, poetry, machinery, vacation, scenery etc.

45. A
Use "whom" in the objective case, and use "who" a subjective case.

46. A
Use a singular verb with a plural noun that refers to a specific amount or quantity that is considered as a whole (dozen, hundred score etc).

47. A
Will is used in the second or third person (they, he, she and you), while shall is used in the first person (I and we). Both verbs are used to express futurity.

48. A
Use a plural verb for nouns like measles, tongs, trousers, riches, scissors etc.

49. C
Always use the singular verb form for nouns like politics, wages, mathematics, innings, news, advice, summons, furniture, information, poetry, machinery, vacation, scenery etc.

50. A
Use a singular verb with either, each, neither, everyone and many.

Basic Math Multiple-Choice Strategy

How to Answer Basic Math Questions - the Basics

First, read the problem, but not the answers.

Work through the problem first and come up with your own answers. Hopefully, you should find your answer among the choices.

If no answer matches the one you got, re-check your math, but this time, use a different method. In math, there are different ways to solve a problem.

Math Multiple Choice Strategy

The two strategies for working with basic math multiple choice are Estimation and Elimination.

Estimation is just as it sounds - try to estimate an approximate answer first. Then look at the choices.

Elimination is probably the most powerful strategy for answering multiple choice.

Eliminate obviously incorrect answers and narrowing the possible choices.

Here are a few basic math examples of how this works.

Solve 2/3 + 5/12

    a. 9/17

    b. 3/11

    c. 7/12

    d. 1 1/12

First estimate the answer. 2/3 is more than half and 5/12 is about half, so the answer is going to be very close to 1.

Next, Eliminate. Choice A is about 1/2 and can be eliminated, choice B is very small, less than 1/2 and can be eliminated. Choice C is close to 1/2 and can be eliminated. Leaving only choice D, which is just over 1.

Work through the solution, find a common denominator and add. The correct answer is 1 1/12, so Choice D is correct.

Let's look at another example:

Solve 4/5 − 2/3

    a. 2/2

    b. 2/13

    c. 1

    d. 2/15

First, quickly estimate the answer. 4/5 is very close to 1, and 2/3 more than half, so the answer is going to be less than 1/2.

Choice A can be eliminated right away, because it is 1. Choice C can be eliminated for the same reason.

Next, look at the denominators. Since 5 and 3 don't go into 13, choice B can be eliminated as well. That leaves choice D. Checking the answer, the common denominator will be 15. So the answer is 2/15 and choice D is correct.

Answer Sheet

	A	B	C	D	E		A	B	C	D	E
1	○	○	○	○	○	21	○	○	○	○	○
2	○	○	○	○	○	22	○	○	○	○	○
3	○	○	○	○	○	23	○	○	○	○	○
4	○	○	○	○	○	24	○	○	○	○	○
5	○	○	○	○	○	25	○	○	○	○	○
6	○	○	○	○	○						
7	○	○	○	○	○						
8	○	○	○	○	○						
9	○	○	○	○	○						
10	○	○	○	○	○						
11	○	○	○	○	○						
12	○	○	○	○	○						
13	○	○	○	○	○						
14	○	○	○	○	○						
15	○	○	○	○	○						
16	○	○	○	○	○						
17	○	○	○	○	○						
18	○	○	○	○	○						
19	○	○	○	○	○						
20	○	○	○	○	○						

Basic Math Strategy Practice Questions

1. Solve 1/4 + 11/16

    a. 9/16
    b. 1 1/16
    c. 11/16
    d. 15/16

2. Solve 7/11 + 3/11

    a. 6/11
    b. 9/11
    c. 10/11
    d. 4/11

3. Solve 5/9 + 2/9

    a. 6/11
    b. 1 3/7
    c. 7/18
    d. 7/9

4. Solve 3/12 + 11/12

    a. 6/12
    b. 1/6
    c. 1 1/6
    d. 1 3/12

5. Solve 13/16 − 1/4

    a. 1
    b. 12/12
    c. 9/16
    d. 7/16

6. Solve 17/23 − 15/23

    a. 2
    b. 1/11
    c. 2/13
    d. 2/23

7. Solve 13/15 − 7/15

    a. 3/5
    b. 7/15
    c. 2/5
    d. 6

8. 33/49 − 23/49

    a. 10/49
    b. 11/49
    c. 10
    d. 13/23

9. Solve 3/4 X 5/11

    a. 2/15
    b. 10/44
    c. 3/19
    d. 15/44

10. Solve 6/10 x 5/16

    a. 4/15
    b. 3/16
    c. 2 1/3
    d. 2/7

11. Solve 3/7 x 4/7

    a. 6/27
    b. 12/49
    c. 3/19
    d. 2/7

12. Solve 4/5 x 2/5

    a. 5/21
    b. 6/25
    c. 8/25
    d. 1 3/5

13. Solve 5/8 ÷ 2/3

    a. 15/16
    b. 10/24
    c. 5/12
    d. 1 2/5

14. Solve 11/20 ÷ 9/20

    a. 99/20
    b. 4 19/20
    c. 1 2/9
    d. 1 1/9

15. Solve 7.25 x 0.5

    a. 3.625
    b. 3.526
    c. 36.25
    d. 35.25

16. Solve 21.02 x 0.34

    a. 71.468
    b. 7.1468
    c. 7.48
    d. 714.68

17. Solve 3.4 ÷ 1.7

    a. 12.05
    b. 9.25
    c. 8.3
    d. 2

18. Solve 2.4 + 3.9

    a. 6.3
    b. 7.3
    c. 5.3
    d. 6.13

19. Solve 3.34 + 2.13

    a. 54.7
    b. 5.57
    c. 5.47
    d. 54.7

20. Solve 42.87 + 26.401

    a. 9.033
    b. 90.33
    c. 73.03
    d. 69.271

21. Solve 6.363 - 1.602

    a. 4.011
    b. 4.761
    c. 47.61
    d. 3.761

22. Solve 67.54 – 43.45

    a. 24.09
    b. 24.19
    c. 24.019
    d. 23.09

23. Convert 75% to decimal

    a. 0.0075
    b. 0.075
    c. 0.75
    d. 7.5

24. Convert 39% to decimal

    a. 0.309
    b. 0.039
    c. 3.9
    d. 0.39

25. What is 25% of 135?

    a. 33.75
    b. 25
    c. 60
    d. 45.35

Answer Key

1. D
Since 9 is less than 11, you can eliminate choice A because an addition problem means that the final number won't be less than one of the initial numbers in the problem. And since 11 is equal to 11, you can eliminate choice C, based on that the sum would be a higher number than the ones you started out with.

Narrowing it down between choice B and D. From the two numbers, you can see that something over a whole number is going to be too high, which just leaves choice D.

Do the calculations to confirm.
A common denominator is needed, a number which both 4 and 16 will divide into. So, (4 + 11)/16 = 15/16

2. C
Since 4, 6, and 9 are all less than the sum of 7 + 3, you can eliminate choice A, B, and D.

Do the calculations to confirm.
Since the denominators are the same, we can just add the numerators, so (7 + 3)/11 = 10/11

3. D
You can eliminate choices A and B right away, since 9 does not go in to 11 or 7, so even if you needed to find a common denominator, neither one of those would be what you were looking for.

9 does go into 18, but it would mean you'd have to multiply everything by 2, and that would be equal to more than 7 when you added the numerators together.

Do the calculations to confirm. Since the denominators are the same, we can just add the numerators, so (5 + 2)/9 = 7/9

4. C
Choice A can be eliminated because 11/12 by itself is more than one half. Choice B can be eliminated because it is so

close to being 0, that 11/12 almost being a whole number means it cannot be 1/6.

Do the calculations to confirm.
Since the denominators are the same, we can just add the numerators, so (3+11)/12 = 14/12 = 1 2/12 = 1 1/6

5. C
Choices A and B can both be eliminated because that are 1 and the difference of two fractions is not going to be 1.

Do the calculations to confirm.
A common denominator' is needed, number which both 16 and 4 will divide into. So 1(3 - 4)/16 = 9/16

6. D
Choice A can be eliminated because 2 is a whole number, which would not be the difference between two subtracted fractions. Choices B and C can be eliminated since neither 11 or 13 go into 23.

Do the calculations to confirm.
Since the denominators are the same, subtract the numerators, so (17 - 15)/23 = 2/23

7. C
You can eliminate choice D because it is a whole number. Since choice B is the same as one of the fractions in the problem, you can eliminate that, since subtracting it is not going to equal a number in the problem.

Do the calculations to confirm.
Since the denominators are the same, subtract the numerators, so (13 - 7)/15 = 6/15 = 2/5

8. A
Choice C can be eliminated as it is a whole number. Choice D can be eliminated because 23 does not go evenly in to 49.

Do the calculations to confirm.
Since the denominators are the same, subtract the numerators, so (33 - 23)/49 = 10/49

9. D
Since 15 and 19 are not common denominators with 4 or 11, choices A and C can be eliminated.

Do the calculations to confirm.
Since there are no common numerators and denominators to cancel out, multiply the numerators and then the denominators. So 3 x 5/4 x 11 = 15/44

10. B
Choice C can be eliminated because multiplying fractions does not give whole numbers. 15 and 7 are not common denominators with 10 or 16, so choices A and D can be eliminated as well.

Do the calculations to confirm.
Since there are common numerators and denominators to cancel out, 6/10 x 5/16 to get 6/2 x 1/16 = 3/2 x 1/8, and multiply numerators and denominators to get 3/16

11. B
Choice D can be eliminated because 2 is less than the product of 3 and 4. Since 7 doesn't go in to 27 or 19, choices A and C can be eliminated.

Do the calculations to confirm.
Since there are no common numerators and denominators to cancel out, we simply multiply the numerators and then the denominators. So 3 x 4/7 x 7 = 12/49

12. C
Since there are no common numerators and denominators to cancel out, we simply multiply the numerators and then the denominators. So 4 x 2/5 x 5 = 8/25

Since multiplying fractions doesn't come out as whole numbers, choice D can be eliminated. Since 5 does not divide evenly into 21, choice A can be eliminated.

13. A
Choice D can be eliminated because it is a number greater than 1. Since dividing fractions is just flipping one and multiplying by the other, choice C can be eliminated since 5 as the

numerator is too small. Since you have to flip the second fraction, choice B can be eliminated as well, as that's just multiplying straight across.

Do the calculations to confirm.
To divide fractions, we multiply the first fraction with the inverse of the second fraction. Therefore 5/8 x 3/2 = 15/16

14. C
Choice A can be eliminated because 99 is the produce of 11 and 9, which would not be multiplied in this problem. Choice B can be eliminated because 4 is too high of a number.

Do the calculations to confirm.
11/20 x 20/9 = 11/1 x 1/9 = 11/9 = 1 2/9

15. A
When multiplying decimals, there should be as many numbers behind the decimal place in the answer, as the sum of the ones in the initial problem, choices C and D can be eliminated. Since it's a multiple of 5, the last number would be 5 and not 6, eliminating choice B.

Do the calculations to confirm.
7.25 x 0.5 = 3.625

16. B
When multiplying decimals, there should be as many numbers behind the decimal place in the answer, as the sum of the ones in the initial problem, choices A C, and D can be eliminated.

Do the calculations to confirm.
21.02 x 0.34 = 7.1468

17. D
Since the estimate of this would be around 1.5, choices A, B, and C are all too high to be the answer.

Do the calculations to confirm.
3.4 ÷ 1.7 = 2

18. A
A quick estimate of equation would be about 6. Choice B is too high and can be eliminated. Choice C is too low, and can be eliminated.

Do the calculations to confirm.
2.4 + 3.9 = 6.3

19. C
A quick estimate would be about 5, which would make choices A and D too high to be the answer.

Do the calculations to confirm.
3.34 + 2.13 = 5.47

20. D
Choice A is too small to be the sum of the two larger numbers and can be eliminated. The estimate of this problem would be about 70, so choices B and C would be too high of a sum.

Do the calculations to confirm.
42.87 + 26.401 = 69.271

21. B
Choice C can be eliminated as it is larger than the starting numbers. 1.602 is about half of 3, so you can eliminate choice D for being too small of a number.

Do the calculations to confirm.
6.363 - 1.602 = 4.761

22. A
Choice C can be eliminated because there are too many numbers after the decimal place.

Do the calculations to confirm.
67.54 – 43.45 = 24.09

23. C
Since 75% can also be written as 75/100, choice D can be eliminated because 75/100 cannot be a whole number. Choices A and B are too small of numbers to be 75/100.

Do the calculations to confirm.

To convert percent to decimal, simply divide the decimal by 100 or move the decimal point 2 places to the left. Therefore, 75 ÷ 100 = 0.75

24. D
Since you can write 39% as 39/100, choice C can be eliminated because a part of 100 will not be a whole number. Choice B is too small of a number to be 39/100.

Do the calculations to confirm.
To convert percent to decimal, simply divide the decimal by 100 or move the decimal point 2 places to the left. Therefore, 39 ÷ 100 = 0.39

25. A
Choice C is close to about 50% of 135, so it can be eliminated. Choice B is 25% of 100, so it can be eliminated as well. Choice D is close to 50 and would be about 33% of 135, leaving you with choice A.

Do the calculations to confirm.
25/100 x 135 = 25 x 1.35 = 33.75

Basic math Video Tutorials

https://www.test-preparation.ca/basic-math-video-tutorials/

Fraction Tips, Tricks and Shortcuts

When you are writing an exam, time is precious, so anything you can do to answer questions faster is a real advantage.

Here are some ideas, shortcuts, tips and tricks that can speed up answering fraction problems.

Remember that a fraction is just a number which names a portion of something. For instance, instead of having a whole pie, a fraction says you have a part of a pie--such as a half of one or a fourth of one.

Two numbers make up a fraction. The number on top is the numerator. The number on the bottom is the denominator.

To remember which is which, just remember that "denominator" and "down" both start with a "d." And the "downstairs" number is the denominator. So for instance, in ½, the numerator is 1, and the denominator (or "downstairs") number is 2.

Adding Fractions

It's easy to add two fractions if they have the same denominator. Just add the digits on top and leave the bottom one the same: $1/10 + 6/10 = 7/10$.

It's the same with subtracting fractions with the same denominator: $7/10 - 6/10 = 1/10$.

Adding and subtracting fractions with different denominators is a little more complicated.

First, you have to arrange the fractions so they have the same denominators.

The easiest way to do this is to multiply the denominators: For

2/5 + 1/2 multiply 5 by 2. Now you have a denominator of 10.

But now you have to change the top numbers too. Since you multiplied the 5 in 2/5 by 2, you also multiply the 2 by 2, to get 4. So the first fraction is now 4/10.

In the second fraction, you multiplied the denominator by 5, you have to multiply the numerator by 5 also, to get 5/10.

Now you have 4/10 + 5/10 and you can add 5 and 4 to get 9/10.

Simplest Form

To reduce a fraction to its simplest form, you have to arrange the numerator and denominator so the only common factor is 1.

Think of it this way:

Let's take an example: The fraction 2/10.

This is not reduced to its simplest terms because there is a number that will divide evenly into both: 2. We want to make it so that the only number that will divide evenly into both is 1.

Divide the top and bottom by 2 to get the new, reduced fraction - 1/5.

Multiplying Fractions

This is the easiest of all: Just multiply the two top numbers and then multiply the two bottom numbers.

Here is an example,

2/5 X 2/3

First, multiply the numerators: 2 X 2 = 4

then multiply the denominators: 5 X 3 = 15

Your answer is 4/15.

Dividing Fractions

Dividing fractions is easy if you remember a simple trick - first turn the second fraction upside down - then multiply!

Here is an example:

7/8 X 1/2

Turn the second fraction upside down:

7/8 X 2/1

then multiply:

(7 X 2) / (8 X 1) = 14/8

Converting Fractions to Decimals

There are a couple of ways to convert fractions to decimals. The first, which is the fastest -- is to memorize some basic fraction facts.

> 1/100 is "one hundredth," expressed as a decimal, it's .01.
>
> 1/50 is "two hundredths," expressed as a decimal, it's .02.
>
> 1/25 is "one twenty-fifth" or "four hundredths," expressed as a decimal, it's .04.
>
> 1/20 is "one twentieth" or ""five hundredths," expressed as a decimal, it's .05.
>
> 1/10 is "one tenth," expressed as a decimal, it's .1.
>
> 1/8 is "one eighth," or "one hundred twenty-five thousandths," expressed as a decimal, it's .125.
>
> 1/5 is "one fifth," or "two tenths," expressed as a decimal, it's .2.
>
> 1/4 is "one fourth" or "twenty-five hundredths," ex-

pressed as a decimal, it's .25.

1/3 is "one third" or "thirty-three hundredths," expressed as a decimal, it's .33.

1/2 is "one half" or "five tenths," expressed as a decimal, it's .5.

3/4 is "three fourths," or "seventy-five hundredths," expressed as a decimal, it's .75.

Of course, if you're no good at memorization, another good technique for converting a fraction to a decimal is to manipulate it so that the fraction's denominator is 10, 100, 1000, or some other power of 10.

Here's an example: We'll start with three quarters. What is the first number in the 4 "times table" that you can multiply and get a multiple of 10? Can you multiply 4 by something to get 10? No. Can you multiply it by something to get 100? Yes! 4 X 25 is 100.

So multiply the numerator by 25, which is 75 over 100

We know fractions are really a division problem, and we also know that dividing by 100, means we move the decimal 2 places to the left.

So, 75 over 100 = .75

Lets try another example - Convert one fifth to a decimal.

First find a power of 10 that 5 goes into evenly, which is 2.

Multiply the numerator and denominator by 2, which is

two tenths.

Dividing 2 by 10 means we move the decimal place 1 place to the left.

So 1/5 = 0.5

Converting Fractions to Percent

Here is a quick method to convert fraction to percent and a strategy for answering on a multiple choice test that will save you valuable exam time.

First, remember that a fraction is a division problem: you're dividing the bottom number into the top.

Taking an example, convert 2/3 into percent.

The first method is to multiple the numerator by 100 and divide. So,

(2 X 100) / 2 = 100/3 = 66.66

Add a % sign and you have the answer, 66.66%

If you're doing these conversions on a multiple-choice test, here's an idea that might be even easier and faster. Let's say you have a fraction of 1/8 and you're asked to convert to percent.

Since we know that "percent" means hundredths, ask yourself what number we can multiply 8 by to get 100. Since there is no number, ask what number gets us close to 100.

That number is 12: 8 X 12 = 96. So it gets us a little less than 100. Now, whatever you do to the denominator, you have to do to the numerator. Let's multiply 1 X 12 and we get 12. However, since 96 is a little less than 100, we know that our answer will be a little MORE than 12%.

Look at the choices and eliminate the obvious wrong choices. So if your possible answers on the multiple-choice test are these:

a) 8.5% b) 19% c) 12.5% d) 25%

then we know the answer is c) 12.5%, because it's a little MORE than the 12 we got in our math problem above.

Here all the choices except choice C 12.5% can be eliminated.

You don't have to know the exact correct answer, just enough to estimate, then eliminate the obviously wrong answers.

This was an easy example to demonstrate the strategy, but don't be fooled! You probably won't get such an easy question on your exam. By estimating your answer quickly, then eliminating obviously incorrect choices immediately, you save precious exam time.

Decimal Tips, Tricks and Shortcuts

Converting Decimals to Fractions

Converting decimals to fractions is easy if you say it the right way! If you say "point one" or "point 25," you'll have trouble.

But if you say, "one tenth" and "twenty-five hundredths," then you have already solved it! That's because, if you know your fractions, you know that "one tenth" looks like this: 1/10. And "twenty-five hundredths" looks like this: 25/100.

Even if you have digits before the decimal, such as 3.4, learning how to say the word will help you with the conversion into a fraction. It's not "three point four," it's "three and four tenths." Knowing this, you know that the fraction which looks like "three and four tenths" is 3 4/10.

The conversion is not complete until you reduce the fraction to its lowest terms: It's not 25/100, but 1/4.

Converting Decimals to Percent

Changing a decimal to a percent is easy if you remember one thing: multiply by 100.

For example, if you start with .45, simply multiply it by 100 for 45. Then add the % sign to the end - 45%.

Think of it way: take out the decimal point, add a percent sign on the opposite side. In other words, the decimal on the left is replaced by the % on the right.

It doesn't work quite that easily if the decimal is in the middle of the number. For example, 3.7. Here, take out the decimal in the middle and replace it with a 0 % at the end. So 3.7 converted to decimal is 370%.

Percent Tips, Tricks and Shortcuts

Percent problems are not nearly as scary as they appear, if you remember this neat trick:

Draw a cross as in:

Portion	Percent
Whole	100

In the upper left, write PORTION. In the bottom left write WHOLE. In the top right, write PERCENT and in the bottom right, write 100. Whatever your problem is, you will leave blank the unknown, and fill in the other four parts. For example, let's suppose your problem is: Find 10% of 50. Since we know the 10% part, we put 10 in the percent corner. Since the whole number in our problem is 50, we put that in the corner marked whole. You always put 100 underneath the percent, so we leave it as is, which leaves only the top left corner blank. This is where we'll put our answer. Now simply multiply the two corner numbers that are NOT 100. Here, it's 10 X 50. That gives us 500. Now divide this by the remaining corner, or 100, to get a final answer of 5. 5 is the number that goes in the upper-left corner, and is your final solution.

Another hint to remember: Percents are the same thing as hundredths in decimals. So .45 is the same as 45 hundredths or 45 percent.

Converting Percents to Decimals

Percents are just a type of decimal, so it should be no surprise that converting between the two is actually fairly simple. Here are a few tricks and shortcuts to keep in mind:

- Remember that percent literally means "per 100" or "for every 100." So when you speak of 30% you're saying 30 for every 100 or the fraction 30/100. In basic math, you learned that fractions that have 10 or 100 as the denominator can easily be turned to a decimal. 30/100 is thirty hundredths, or expressed as a decimal, .30.
- Another way to look at it: To convert a percent to a decimal, simply divide the number by 100. So for instance, if the percent is 47%, divide 47 by 100. The result will be .47. Get rid of the % mark and you're done.
- Remember that the easiest way of dividing by 100 is by moving your decimal two spots to the left.

Converting Percents to Fractions

Converting percents to fractions is easy. After all, a percent is just a type of fraction; it tells you what part of 100 that you're talking about. Here are some simple ideas for making the conversion from a percent to a fraction:

- If the percent is a whole number -- say 34% -- then simply write a fraction with 100 as the denominator (the bottom number). Then put the percentage itself on top. So 34% becomes 34/100.
- Now reduce as you would reduce any percent. In this case, by dividing 2 into 34 and 2 into 100, you get 17/50.
- If your percent is not a whole number -- say 3.4% --then convert it to a decimal expressed as hundredths. 3.4 is the same as 3.40 (or 3 and forty hundredths). Now ask yourself how you would express "three and forty hundredths" as a fraction. It would, of course, be 3 40/100. Reduce this and it becomes 3 2/5.

Word Problem Multiple-Choice Strategy

How to Solve Word Problems

Do you know what the biggest tip for solving word problems is?

Practice regularly and systematically.

Sounds simple and easy right? Yes it is, and yes it really does work.

Word problems are a way of thinking and require you to translate a real-world problem into mathematical terms.

Some math teachers say that learning how to think mathematically is the main reason for teaching word problems.

So what does that mean?

Studying word problems and math in general requires a logical and mathematical frame of mind. The only way you can get this is by practicing regularly, which means every day.

It is critical that you practice word problems every day for the 5 days before the exam as the absolute minimum.

If you practice and miss a day, you have lost the mathematical frame of mind and the benefit of your previous practice is gone. You must start all over again.

Everything is important.

All the information given in the problem has some purpose. There is no unnecessary information! Word problems are typically around 50 words in 2 or 3 sentences.

Often, the relationships are complicated. To explain everything, every word counts.

Make sure that you use every piece of information.

7 steps to solving word problems

Step 1 – Read through the problem at least three times. The first reading should be a quick scan, and the next two readings should be done slowly to find answers to these questions:

> What does the problem ask? (Usually located at the end)

Mark all information and underline all important words or phrases.

Step 2 – Draw a picture. Use arrows, circles, lines, whatever works for you. This makes the problem real.

A favorite word problem is something like, 1 train leaves Station A travelling at 100 km/hr and another train leaves Station B travelling at 60 km/hr. ...

Draw a line, the two stations, and the two trains at either end.

Depending on the question, make a table with a blank portion to show information you don't know.

Step 3 – Assign a single letter to represent each unknown.

You may want to note the unknown that each letter represents so you don't get confused.

Step 4 – Translate the information into an equation.

Remember that the main problem with word problems is

that they are not expressed in regular math equations. Your ability to identify correctly the variables and translate the information into an equation determines your ability to solve the problem.

Step 5 – Check the equation to see if it looks like regular equations that you are used to seeing and whether it looks sensible.

Does the equation appear to represent the information in the question? Take note that you may need to rewrite some formulas needed to solve the word problem equation.

Step 6 – Use algebra rules to solve the equation.

Simplify each side of the equation by removing parentheses and combining like terms.

Use addition or subtraction to isolate the variable term on one side of the equation. If a number crosses to the other side of the equation, the sign changes to the opposite -- for example positive to negative.

Use multiplication or division to solve for the variable. What you to once side of the equation you must do for the other.

Where there are multiple unknowns you will need to use elimination or substitution methods to resolve all the equations.

Step 7 – Check your final answers to see if they make sense with the information given in the problem.

For example, if the word problem involves a discount, the final price should be less or if a product was taxed then the final answer has to cost more.

Types of Word problems

Word problems can be classified into 12 types. Below are examples of each type with a complete solution. Some types of Word problems can be solved quickly using multiple-choice strategies and some cannot. Always look for ways to estimate the answer and then eliminate choices.

1. Age

A girl is 10 years older than her brother. By next year, she will be twice the age of her brother. What are their ages now?

    a. 25, 15
    b. 19, 9
    c. 21, 11
    d. 29, 19

Solution: B

We will assume that the girl's age is "a" and her brother's is "b." This means that based on the information in the first sentence,
$a = 10$

Next year, she will be twice her brother's age, which gives
$a + 1 = 2(b+1)$

We need to solve for one unknown factor and then use the answer to solve for the other. To do this we substitute the value of "a" from the first equation into the second equation. This gives

$10 + b + 1 = 2b + 2$
$11 + b = 2b + 2$
$11 - 2 = 2b - b$
$b = 9$

$9 = b$ this means that her brother is 9 years old.
Solving for the girl's age in the first equation gives

$a = 10 + 9$
$a = 19$ the girl is aged 19. So, the girl is aged 19 and the boy is 9

2. Distance or speed

Two boats travel down a river towards the same destination, starting at the same time. One boat is traveling at 52 km/hr, and the other boat at 43 km/hr. How far apart will they be after 40 minutes?

    a. 46.67 km
    b. 19.23 km
    c. 6.03 km
    d. 14.39 km

Solution: C

After 40 minutes, the first boat will have traveled = 52 km/hr x 40 minutes/60 minutes = 34.7 km

After 40 minutes, the second boat will have traveled = 43 km/hr x 40/60 minutes = 28.66 km

Difference between the two boats will be 34.7 km – 28.66 km = 6.03 km

Multiple-Choice Strategy

First estimate the answer. The first boat is travelling 9 km. faster than the second, for 40 minutes, which is 2/3 of an hour. 2/3 of 9 = 6, as a rough guess of the distance apart.

Choices A, B and D can be eliminated right away.

3. Ratio

The instructions in a cookbook states that 700 grams of flour must be mixed in 100 ml of water, and 0.90 grams of salt added. A cook however has just 325 grams of flour. What is the quantity of water and salt that he should use?

    a. 0.41 grams and 46.4 ml
    b. 0.45 grams and 49.3 ml
    c. 0.39 grams and 39.8 ml
    d. 0.25 grams and 40.1 ml

Solution: A

The Cookbook states 700 grams of flour, but the cook only has 325. The first step is to determine the percentage of flour he has 325/700 x 100 = 46.4%
That means that 46.4% of all other items must also be used.
46.4% of 100 = 46.4 ml of water
46.4% of 0.90 = 0.41 grams of salt.

Multiple-Choice Strategy

The recipe calls for 700 grams of flour but the cook only has 325, which is just less than half, the amount of water and salt are going to be about half.

Choices C and D can be eliminated right away. Choice B is very close so be careful. Looking closely at Choice B, it is exactly half, and since 325 is slightly less than half of 700, it can't be correct.

Choice A is correct.

4. Percent

An agent received $6,685 as his commission for selling a property. If his commission was 13% of the selling price, how much was the property?

   a. $68,825
   b. $121,850
   c. $49,025
   d. $51,423

Solution: D

Let's assume that the property price is x
That means from the information given, 13% of x = 6,685
Solve for x,
x = 6685 x 100/13 = $51,423

Multiple-Choice Strategy

The commission, 13%, is just over 10%, which is easier to work with. Round up $6685 to $6700, and multiple by 10 for an approximate answer. 10 X 6700 = $67,000. You can do

this in your head. Choice B is much too big and can be eliminated. Choice C is too small and can be eliminated. Choices A and D are left and good possibilities.
Do the calculations to make the final choice.

5. Sales & Profit

A store owner buys merchandise for $21,045. He transports them for $3,905 and pays his staff $1,450 to stock the merchandise on his shelves. If he does not incur further costs, how much does he need to sell the items to make $5,000 profit?

    a. $32,500
    b. $29,350
    c. $32,400
    d. $31,400

Solution: D

Total cost of the items is $21,045 + $3,905 + $1,450 = $26,400
Total cost is now $26,400 + $5000 profit = $31,400

Multiple-Choice Strategy

Round off and add the numbers up in your head quickly. 21,000 + 4,000 + 1500 = 26500. Add in 5000 profit for a total of 31500.

Choice B is too small and can be eliminated. Choice C and Choice A are too large and can be eliminated.

6. Tax/Income

A woman earns $42,000 per month and pays 5% tax on her monthly income. If the Government increases her monthly taxes by $1,500, what is her income after tax?

    a. $38,400
    b. $36,050
    c. $40,500
    d. $39, 500

Solution: A

Initial tax on income was 5/100 x 42,000 = $2,100
$1,500 was added to the tax to give $2,100 + 1,500 = $3,600
Income after tax left is $42,000 - $3,600 = $38,400

7. Interest

A man invests $3000 in a 2-year term deposit that pays 3% interest per year. How much will he have at the end of the 2-year term?

    a. $5,200
    b. $3,020
    c. $3,182.7
    d. $3,000

Solution: C

This is a compound interest problem. The funds are invested for 2 years and interest is paid yearly, so in the second year, he will earn interest on the interest paid in the first year.

3% interest in the first year = 3/100 x 3,000 = $90
At end of first year, total amount = 3,000 + 90 = $3,090
Second year = 3/100 x 3,090 = 92.7.
At end of second year, total amount = $3090 + $92.7 = $3,182.7

8. Averaging

The average weight of 10 books is 54 grams. 2 more books were added and the average weight became 55.4. If one of the 2 new books added weighed 62.8 g, what is the weight of the other?

    a. 44.7 g
    b. 67.4 g
    c. 62 g
    d. 52 g

Solution: C

Total weight of 10 books with average 54 grams will be=10×54=540 g
Total weight of 12 books with average 55.4 will be=55.4×12=664.8 g
So total weight of the remaining 2 will be= 664.8 – 540 = 124.8 g
If one weighs 62.8, the weight of the other will be= 124.8 g – 62.8 g = 62 g

Multiple-Choice Strategy

Averaging problems can be estimated by looking at which direction the average goes. If additional items are added and the average goes up, the new items much be greater than the average. If the average goes down after new items are added, the new items must be less than the average.

Here, the average is 54 grams and 2 books are added which increases the average to 55.4, so the new books must weight more than 54 grams.

Choices A and D can be eliminated right away.

9. Probability

A bag contains 15 marbles of various colors. If 3 marbles are white, 5 are red and the rest are black, what is the probability of randomly picking out a black marble from the bag?

    a. 7/15
    b. 3/15
    c. 1/5
    d. 4/15

Solution: A

Total marbles = 15
Number of black marbles = 15 − (3 + 5) = 7
Probability of picking out a black marble = 7/15

10. Two Variables

A company paid a total of $2850 to book for 6 single rooms and 4 double rooms in a hotel for one night. Another company paid $3185 to book for 13 single rooms for one night in the same hotel. What is the cost for single and double rooms in that hotel?

    a. single= $250 and double = $345
    b. single= $254 and double = $350
    c. single = $245 and double = $305
    d. single = $245 and double = $345

Solution: D

We can determine the price of single rooms from the information given of the second company. 13 single rooms = 3185.
One single room = 3185 / 13 = 245
The first company paid for 6 single rooms at $245. 245 x 6 = $1470
Total amount paid for 4 double rooms by first company = $2850 - $1470 = $1380
Cost per double room = 1380 / 4 = $345

11. Geometry

The length of a rectangle is 5 in. more than its width. The perimeter of the rectangle is 26 in. What is the width and length of the rectangle?

    a. width = 6 inches, Length = 9 inches
    b. width = 4 inches, Length = 9 inches
    c. width =4 inches, Length = 5 inches
    d. width = 6 inches, Length = 11 inches

Solution: B

Formula for perimeter of a rectangle is 2(L + W)
p=26, so 2(L+W) = p
The length is 5 inches more than the width, so
2(w + 5) + 2w = 26
2w + 10 + 2w = 26
2w + 2w = 26 - 10
4w = 18

W = 16/4 = 4 inches

L is 5 inches more than w, so L = 5 + 4 = 9 inches.

12. Totals and fractions

A basket contains 125 oranges, mangos and apples. If 3/5 of the fruits in the basket are mangos and only 2/5 of the mangos are ripe, how many ripe mangos are there in the basket?

    a. 30
    b. 68
    c. 55
    d. 47

Solution: A
Number of mangos in the basket is 3/5 x 125 = 75
Number of ripe mangos = 2/5 x 75 = 30

Answer Sheet

	A	B	C	D
1	○	○	○	○
2	○	○	○	○
3	○	○	○	○
4	○	○	○	○
5	○	○	○	○
6	○	○	○	○
7	○	○	○	○
8	○	○	○	○
9	○	○	○	○
10	○	○	○	○

Practice Questions

1. The average weight of 13 students in a class of 15 (two were absent that day) is 42 kg. When the remaining two are weighed, the average became 42.7 kg. If one of the remaining students weighs 48 kg., how much does the other weigh?

   a. 44.7 kg.
   b. 45.6 kg.
   c. 46.5 kg.
   d. 41.4 kg.

2. Brad has agreed to buy everyone a Coke. Each drink costs $1.89, and there are 5 friends. Estimate Brad's cost.

   a. $7
   b. $8
   c. $10
   d. $12

3. At the beginning of 2009, Madalyn invested $5,000 in a savings account. The account pays 4% interest per year. How much will Madalyn have in the account in 2 years?

   a. $5,408
   b. $5,200
   c. $5,110
   d. $7,000

4. The cost of waterproofing canvas is .50 a square yard. What's the total cost for waterproofing a canvas truck cover that is 15' x 24'?

    a. $18.00

    b. $6.67

    c. $180.00

    d. $20.00

5. John is a barber and receives 40% of the amount paid by each of his customers, and all of any tips paid to him. If a man pays $8.50 for a haircut and tips $1.30, how much money does John receive?

    a. $3.92

    b. $4.70

    c. $5.70

    d. $6.40

6. Two trains start their journey at the same time, one with average speed of 72 km/hr and other with 52 km/hr. How far apart are the trains after 20 minutes?

    a. 6.67 km

    b. 17.33 km

    c. 24.3 km

    d. 41.33 km

7. John purchased a jacket at a 7% discount. He had a membership and received an additional discount of 1.6%. If he paid $425, what is the retail price of the jacket?

    a. $448

    b. $460

    c. $466

    d. $472

8. A store sells stereos for $545. If 15% of the cost was added to the price as value added tax, what is the total cost?

   a. $490.4
   b. $626.75
   c. $575.00
   d. $590.15

9. A car covers a certain distance in 3.5 hours at an average speed of 60 km/hr. How much time in hours will a motorbike take to cover the same distance at an average speed of 40 km/hr?

   a. 4.5
   b. 4.75
   c. 5.25
   d. 5

10. Jim left home for the office at 7:00 am. He reached his office at 7:48 am. How far is his house from office if his average driving speed is 40km/hr?

   a. 32 km
   b. 34 km
   c. 38 km
   d. 40 km

Answer Key

1. C

Total weight of 13 students with average 42 will be = 42 × 13 = 546 kg.
Total weight of 15 students with average 42.7 will be = 42.7 × 15 = 640.5 kg. So total weight of the remaining 2 will be = 640.5 - 546 = 94.5 kg. Weight of the other will be = 94.5 – 48 = 46.5 kg

Multiple-Choice Strategy

When the 2 additional students were added, the average went up, so they must weigh more than the average. Choice D is less than the average so it can be eliminated right away.

2. C

If there are 5 friends and each drink costs $1.89, we can round up to $2 per drink and estimate the total cost at, 5 X $2 = $10.

The actual, cost is 5 X $1.89 = $9.45.

3. A

This is a compound interest problem. Interest is paid out at the end of the first year and added to the account, and then interest is paid on the new total in the second year.

First do a quick calculation in your head, using numbers that are easy to work with. 5000 X 10% = 500 and so 5% will be half of that which is $250. If we ignore the compounding (interest on interest) in the second year, we have an approximate total of $5500, which is a high approximation.

Choice D can be eliminated as much too high, and choice C is too low. Choice B is about the total for one years interest so it can also be eliminated. Choice A is the only choice left.

Do the calculations to confirm.

5000 X 4% = 200
In the second year, 5200 X 4% = 208

So the total at the end of the second year is $5,408.

4. D
This is a square foot cost problem. The problem is to find the total square footage, and the multiply by the cost. Use math shortcuts to calculate the answer in your head. First calculate total square feet, which is 15 * 24 = 360 ft². Next, convert this value to square yards, (1 yards² = 9 ft²) which is 360/9 = 40 yards². At $0.50 per square yard, the total cost is 40•0.50 (or half) = $20.

5. B
Estimate the answer in your head quickly. 40% is close to 50%, which is half. 50% of $8.50 is 4.25 plus tips of $1.30 is 5.55 approximately.

Looking at the options, choices A and D can all be eliminated as too low or too high, leaving choice B and C. C is probably too high, as 5.55 is an approximation and so choice B is looking correct.

Do the calculations to confirm.
8.5 X 40/100 = 3.40 + 1.30 = $4.70.

6. A
First estimate the answer quickly in your head. One train is travelling at 72 km. and the other at 52 km. In one hour they will be 20 km. apart, so in 20 minutes they will be 20/3 = about 6.5 km.

Looking at the options, choices B and C are far to big and can be eliminated. Choice D is closer, but still too large, and can also be eliminated.

Do the calculations to confirm.
Distance traveled by 1st train in 20 minute = (72 km/hr×20 minutes)/60 minutes = 24 km
Distance traveled by 2nd train in 20 minute = (52 km/hr×20 minutes)/60 minutes = 17.33 km
Difference in distance = 24 - 17.33 = 6.67 km

7. C
Make a rough estimate in your head. Use 10% instead of 7%,

so 425 + 10% = 467. Ignore the 1.6% for now and remember this is an estimate on the high side.

Choice A is too small and can be eliminated and choice D is too high and can be eliminated. That leaves choices B and C.

Do the calculations to confirm.
Let the original price be x, then at rate of 7% the discounted price will be = 0.93x
2% discounted amount then will be = 0.02 × 0.93x = 0.0186x
Remaining price = 0.93x - 0.0186x = 0.9114x
This is the amount which John has paid so
0.9114x = 425
x = 425/ 0.9114
x = $466.31

8. B
This question can be estimated in your head with a few shortcuts. 15% is difficult to work with so use 10% and 5%.
10% of 545 = 54.5
5% of 545 = about 27 (half of 10%)
Add them quickly in your head by estimating again. Take 50 + 25 = 75 and add 7 for a rough approximation of 82. The actual number is 81.5.
Add 82 to 545. Again round to easy numbers to work with. take 550 + 82 = 632. Remember this is a high estimate. (The actual figure is 626.5)

Looking at the options, the only choice over 600 is Choice B.

Confirm by doing the calculations.
Actual cost = X, therefore, X = 545 + (545 X 0.15)
X = 545 + 81.75
X = 626.75

9. C
Estimate the answer first. The car is travelling at 60 km. and the motorbike is travelling at 40 km., which is 2/3 (40/60 = 2/3, or 2:3). So the motorcycle will take one-third longer to travel the same distance. If the car took 3.5 hours, the motorbike will take 3.5 + (1/3 of 3.5). 1/3 of 3.5 is going to be about 1.1, or say 1. 3.5 + 1 = 4.5.

Looking at the options, choice D can be eliminated right away. Choice A can be eliminated since it equals our estimate.

Do the calculations to confirm.
The distance covered by the car = 60 X 3.5 = 210 km.
Time required by the motorbike = 210/40 = 5.25 hr.

10. A
Do a quick estimate in your head and see if any options can be eliminated. Jim is travelling for 48 minutes at 40 km. per hour. If he was travelling for one hour, he would cover 40 km. Right away choice D can be eliminated because he is only travelling for a portion of an hour. Choice C, 38 km. is a very unlikely choice because it is so close to 40 and can be eliminated. The answer will be choice A or B.

Do the calculations to confirm.
Time to reach the office = 48 minutes. So if he covers 40 km in 60 minutes, then in 48 minutes, he will cover 48 X 40/60 = 32 km.

How to Prepare for a Test

MOST STUDENTS HIDE THEIR HEADS AND PROCRASTINATE WHEN FACED WITH PREPARING FOR AN EXAM, HOPING THAT SOMEHOW THEY WILL BE SPARED THE AGONY, ESPECIALLY IF IT IS A BIG ONE THAT THEIR FUTURES RELY ON. Avoiding a test is what many students do best and unfortunately, they suffer the consequences because of their lack of preparation.

Test preparation requires strategy and dedication. It is the perfect training ground for a professional life. Besides having several reliable strategies, successful students also has a clear goal and know how to accomplish it. These tried and true concepts have worked well and will make your test preparation easier.

Test Prep and Study Skills Video Tutorials

https://www.test-preparation.ca/video-series-on-test-preparation-multiple-choice-strategies-and-how-to-study/

Take responsibility for your own test preparation.

It is a common - but big - mistake to link your studying to someone else's. Study partners are great, but only if they are reliable. It is your job to be prepared for the test, even if a study partner fails you. Do not allow others to distract you from your goals.

Prioritize the time available to study

When do you learn best, early in the day or at night? Does your mind absorb and retain information most efficiently in small blocks of time, or do you require long stretches to get the most done? It is important to figure out the best blocks of time available to you when you can be the most productive. Try to consolidate activities to allow for longer periods of study time.

Find a quiet place where you will not be disturbed

Do not try to squeeze in quality study time in any old location. Find a quiet place with a minimum of distractions, such as the library, a park or even the laundry room. Good lighting is essential and you need to have comfortable seating and a desk surface large enough to hold your materials. It is probably not a great idea to study in your bedroom. You might be distracted by clothes on the floor, a book you have been planning to read, the telephone or something else. Besides, in the middle of studying, that bed will start to look very comfortable. Whatever you do, avoid using the bed as a place to study since you might fall asleep to avoiding studying!

The exception is flashcards. By far the most productive study time is sitting down and studying and studying only. However, with flashcards you can carry them with you and make use of odd moments, like standing in line or waiting for the bus. This isn't as productive, but it really helps and is definitely worth doing.

Determine what you need to study

Gather together your books, your notes, your laptop and any other materials needed to focus on your study for this exam. Ensure you have everything you need so you don't waste time. Remember paper, pencils and erasers, sticky notes, bottled water and a snack. Keep your phone with you if you need it to find essential information, but keep it turned off so others can't distract you.

Have a positive attitude

It is essential that you approach your studies for the test with an attitude that says you will pass it. And pass it with flying colors! This is one of the most important keys to successful studying. Believing that you are capable helps you to become capable.

The Strategy of Studying

Review class notes

Stay on top of class notes and assignments by reviewing them frequently and regularly and regularly. Re-writing notes can be a terrific study trick, as it helps lock in information. Pay special attention to any comments that have been made by the teacher. If a study guide has been made available as part of the class materials, use it! It will be a valuable tool to use for studying.

Estimate how much time you will need

If you are concerned about the amount of time you have available it is a good idea to set up a schedule so that you do not get bogged down on one section and end without enough time left to study other things. Remember to schedule break time, and use that time for a little exercise or other stress reducing techniques.

Test yourself to determine your weaknesses

Look online for additional assessment and evaluation tools available like practice questions for a particular subject. Visit our website http://www.test-preparation.ca

What Students Say!

Visit our Online Library of student tips and strategies

https://www.test-preparation.ca/test-prep-and-studying-what-students-say/ for test tips and more practice questions. Once you have determined your weaknesses, you can focus on these, and just brush up on the other areas of the exam.

Mental Prep – How to Psych Yourself Up for a Test

Since tests are often a big factor in your final grade or acceptance into a program, it is understandable that taking tests can create a great deal of anxiety for many students. Even students who know they have learned the required material find their minds going blank as they stare at the test booklet. You can avoid test anxiety by preparing yourself mentally. One easy way to overcome that anxiety is to prepare mentally for the test with a few simple techniques.

Do not procrastinate

Study the material for the test when it becomes available, and continue to review the material until the test day. By waiting until the last minute and trying to cram for the test the night before, you actually increase anxiety. This leads to negative self-talk, which becomes self-fulfilling. Telling yourself "I can't learn this. I am going to fail" is a pretty sure indication that you are right.

Positive self-talk.

Positive self-talk drowns out negative self-talk and to increases your confidence level. Whenever you begin feeling overwhelmed or anxious about the test, remind yourself that you have studied enough, you know the material and that you will pass the test. Both negative and positive self-talk are really just your fantasy, so why not choose to be a winner?

Do not compare yourself to others.

Do not compare yourself to other students. Instead, focus on your strengths and weaknesses and prepare accordingly. Regardless of how others perform, your performance is the only one that matters to your grade. Comparing yourself to others increases your anxiety and negative self-talk before the test.

Visualize.

Make a mental image of yourself taking the test. You know the answers and feel relaxed. Visualize doing well on the test and having no problems with the material. Visualizations can increase your confidence and decrease the anxiety you might otherwise feel before the test. Instead of thinking of this as a test, see it as an opportunity to demonstrate what you have learned!

Avoid negativity.

Worry is contagious and viral - once it gets started it builds on itself. Cut it off before it gets to be a problem. Even if you are relaxed and confident, being around anxious, worried classmates might cause you to start feeling anxious. Before the test, tune out the fears of classmates. Feeling anxious and worried before an exam is normal, and every student experiences those feelings at some point. But you cannot allow these feelings to interfere with your performance. Practicing mental preparation techniques and remembering that the test is not the only measure of your academic performance will ease your anxiety and ensure that you perform at your best.

How to Take a Test

EVERYONE KNOWS THAT TAKING AN EXAM IS STRESSFUL, BUT IT DOES NOT HAVE TO BE THAT BAD! There are a few simple things that you can do to increase your score on any type of test. Take a look at these tips and consider how you can incorporate them into your study time.

OK - so you are in the test room - Here is what to do!

Reading the Instructions

This is the most basic point, but one that, surprisingly, many students ignore and it costs big time! Since reading the instructions is one of the most common, and 100% preventable mistakes, we have a whole section just on reading instructions.

Pay close attention to the sample questions. Almost all standardized tests offer sample questions, paired with their correct solutions. Go through these to make sure that you understand what they mean and how they arrived at the correct answer. Do not be afraid to ask the test supervisor for help with a sample that confuses you, or instructions that you are unsure of.

Tips for Reading the Question

We could write pages and pages of tips just on reading the test questions. Here are a few that will help you the most.

- **Think first.** Before you look at the answer, read and think about the question. It is best to try to come up with the correct answer before you look at the options. This way, when the test-writer tries to trick you with a close answer, you will not fall for it.

- **Make it true or false.** If a question confuses you, then look at each answer option and think of it as a "true" "false" question. Select the one that seems most likely to be "true."

- **Mark the Question.** Don't be afraid to mark up the test booklet. Unless you are specifically told not to mark in the booklet, use it to your advantage.

- **Circle Key Words.** As you are reading the question, underline or circle key words. This helps you to focus on the most critical information needed to solve the problem. For example, if the question said, "Which of these is not a synonym for huge?" You might circle "not," "synonym" and "huge." That clears away the clutter and lets you focus on what is important.

- **Always underline these words:** all, none, always, never, most, best, true, false and except.

- **Eliminate.** Elimination is the best strategy for multiple choice answers *and* questions. If you are confused by lengthy questions, cross out anything that you think is irrelevant, obviously wrong, or information that you think is offered to distract you. Elimination is the most valuable strategy!

- **Do not try to read between the lines.** Usually, questions are written to be straightforward, with no deep, underlying meaning. Generally, the simple answer really is the correct answer. Do not over-analyze!

How to Take a Test - The Basics

Some sections of the test are designed to assess your ability to quickly grab the necessary information; this type of exam makes speed a priority. Others are more concerned with your depth of knowledge, and how accurate it is. When you start a new section of the test, look it over to determine whether the test is for speed or accuracy. If the test is for speed (a lot of questions and a short time), your strategy is clear; answer as many questions as quickly as possible.

The TABE© does NOT penalize for wrong answers, so if all else fails, guess and make sure you answer every question.

Every little bit helps

The TABE© test allows four function calculators may be used during the Applied Mathematics portion of the test. . Make sure you know how to use it!

You cannot bring any other materials into the test room. Scratch paper and a pencil are provided. Use them!

Make time your friend

Budget your time from the beginning until you are finished, and stick to it! The amount of time you are permitted for each portion of the test will almost certainly be included in the instructions.

Easy does it

One smart way to tackle a test is to locate the easy questions and answer those first. This is a time-tested strategy that never fails, because it saves you a lot of unnecessary anxiety. First, read the question and decide if you can answer it in less than a minute. If so, complete the question and go to the next one. If not, skip it for now and continue to the next question. By the time you have completed the first pass through this section of the exam, you will have answered a good number of questions. Not only does it boost your confidence, relieve anxiety and kick your memory up a notch, you will know exactly how many questions remain and can allot the rest of your time accordingly. Think of doing the easy questions first as a warm-up!

Do not watch your watch

At best, taking an important exam is an uncomfortable situation. If you are like most people, you might be tempted to subconsciously distract yourself from the task at hand. One of the most common ways is by becoming obsessed with your watch or the wall clock. Do not watch your watch! Take it off and place it on the top corner of your desk, far enough away that you will not be tempted to look at it every two minutes. Better still, turn the watch face away from you. That way, every time you try to sneak a peek, you will be reminded to refocus your attention to the task at hand. Give yourself permission to check your watch or the wall clock after you complete each section. Focus on answering the questions, not on how many minutes have elapsed since you last looked at it.

Divide and conquer

What should you do when you come across a question that is so complicated you may not even be certain what is being asked? As we have suggested, the first time through, skip the question. At some point, you will need to return to it and get it under control. The best way to handle questions that leave you feeling so anxious you can hardly think is by breaking them into manageable pieces. Solving smaller bits is always easier. For complicated questions, divide them into bite-sized pieces and solve these smaller sets separately. Once you understand what the reduced sections are really saying, it will be much easier to put them together and get a handle on the bigger question. This may not work with every question - see below for how to deal with questions you cannot break down.

Reason your way through the toughest questions

If you find that a question is so dense you can't figure out how to break it into smaller pieces, there are a few strategies that might help. First, read the question again and look for hints. Can you re-word the question in one or more different ways? This may give you clues. Look for words that can function as either verbs or nouns, and try to figure out what the questions is asking from the sentence structure. Remember that many nouns in English have several different meanings. While some of those meanings might be related, sometimes they are completely distinct. If reading the sentence one way does not make sense, consider a different definition or meaning for a key word.

The truth is, it is not always necessary to understand a question to arrive at a correct answer! The most successful strategy for multiple choice is Elimination. Frequently, at least one answer is clearly wrong and can be crossed off the list of possible correct answers. Next, look at the remaining answers and eliminate any that are only partially true. You may still have to flat-out guess from time to time, but using the process of elimination will help you make your way to the correct answer more often than not - even when you don't know what the question means!

Do not leave early
Use all the time allotted to you, even if you can't wait to get out of the testing room. Instead, once you have finished, spend the remaining time reviewing your answers. Go back to those questions that were most difficult for you and review your response. Another good way to use this time is to return to multiple-choice questions in which you filled in a bubble. Do a spot check, reviewing every fifth or sixth question to make sure your answer coincides with the bubble you filled in. This is a great way to catch yourself if you made a mistake, skipped a bubble and therefore put all your answers in the wrong bubbles!

Become a super sleuth and look for careless errors. Look for questions that have double negatives or other odd phrasing; they might be an attempt to throw you off. Careless errors on your part might be the result of skimming a question and missing a key word. Words such as "always", "never", "sometimes" , "rarely" and the like can give a strong indication of the answer the question is really seeking. Don't throw away points by being careless!

Just as you budgeted time at the beginning of the test to allow for easy and more difficult questions, be sure to budget sufficient time to review your answers. On essay questions and math questions where you are required to show your work, check your writing to make sure it is legible.

Math questions can be especially tricky. The best way to double check math questions is by figuring the answer using a different method, if possible.

Here is another terrific tip. It is likely that no matter how hard you try, you will have a handful of questions you just are not sure of. Keep them in mind as you read through the rest of the test. If you can't answer a question, looking back over the test to find a different question that addresses the same topic might give you clues.

We know that taking the test has been stressful and you can hardly wait to escape. Just Leaving before you double-check as much as possible can be a quick trip to disaster. Taking a few extra minutes can make the difference between getting a bad grade and a great one. Besides, there will be lots of time to relax and celebrate after the test is turned in.

In the Test Room – What you MUST do!

If you are like the rest of the world, there is almost nothing you would rather avoid than taking a test. Unfortunately, that is not an option if you want to pass. Rather than suffer, consider a few attitude adjustments that might turn the experience from a horrible one to...well, an interesting one! Take a look at these tips. Simply changing how you perceive the experience can change the experience itself.

You have to take the test - you can't change that. What you can change, and the only thing that you can change, is your attitude -so get a grip - you can do it!

Get in the mood

After weeks of studying, the big day has finally arrived. The worst thing you can do to yourself is arrive at the test site feeling frustrated, worried, and anxious. Keep a check on your emotional state. If your emotions are shaky before a test it can determine how well you do on the test. It is extremely important that you pump yourself up, believe in yourself, and use that confidence to get in the mood!

Don't fight reality

Students often resent tests, and with good reason. After all, many people do not test well, and they know the grade they end with does not accurately reflect their true knowledge. It is easy to feel resentful because tests classify students and create categories that just don't seem fair. Face it: Students who are great at rote memorization and not that good at actually analyzing material often score higher than those who might be more creative thinkers and balk at simply memorizing cold, hard facts. It may not be fair, but there it is anyway. Conformity is an asset on tests, and creativity is often a liability. There is no point in wasting time or energy being upset about this reality. Your first step is to accept the reality and get used to it. You will get higher marks when you realize tests do count and that you must give them your best effort. Think about your future and the career that is easier to achieve if you have consistently earned high grades. Avoid negative energy and focus on anything that lifts your enthusiasm and increases your motivation.

Get there early enough to relax

If you are wound up, tense, scared, anxious, or feeling rushed, it will cost you. Get to the exam room early and relax before you go in. This way, when the exam starts, you are comfortable and ready to apply yourself. Of course, you do not want to arrive so early that you are the only one there. That will not help you relax; it will only give you too much time to sit there, worry and get wound up all over again.

If you can, visit the room where you will be taking your exam a few days ahead of time. Having a visual image of the room can be surprisingly calming, because it takes away one of the big 'unknowns'. Not only that, but once you have visited, you know how to get there and will not be worried about getting lost. Furthermore, driving to the test site once lets you know how much time you need to allow for the trip. That means three potential stressors have been eliminated all at once.

Get it down on paper

One advantage of arriving early is that it allows you time to recreate notes. If you spend a lot of time worrying about whether you will be able to remember information like names, dates, places, and mathematical formulas, there is a solution for that. Unless the exam you are taking allows you to use your books and notes, (and very few do) you will have to rely on memory. Arriving early gives to time to tap into your memory and jot down key pieces of information that you know will be asked. Just make certain you are allowed to make notes once you are in the testing site; not all locations will permit it. Once you get your test, on a small piece of paper write down everything you are afraid you will forget. It will take a minute or two but by dumping your worries onto the page you have effectively eliminated a certain amount of anxiety and driven off the panic you feel.

Get comfortable in your chair

Here is a clever technique that releases physical stress and helps you get comfortable, even relaxed in your body. You will tense and hold each of your muscles for just a few seconds. The trick is, you must tense them hard for the technique to work. You might want to practice this technique a few times at home; you do not want an unfamiliar technique to add to your stress just before a test, after all! Once you are at the test site, this exercise can always be done in the rest room or another quiet location.

Start with the muscles in your face then work down your body. Tense, squeeze and hold the muscles for a moment or two. Notice the feel of every muscle as you go down your body. Scowl to tense your forehead, pull in your chin to tense your neck. Squeeze your shoulders down to tense your back. Pull in your stomach all the way back to your ribs, make your lower back tight then stretch your fingers. Tense your leg muscles and calves then stretch your feet and your toes. You should be as stiff as a board throughout your entire body.

Now relax your muscles in reverse starting with your toes. Notice how all the muscles feel as you relax them one by one. Once you have released a muscle or set of muscles, allow them to remain relaxed as you proceed up your body. Focus on how you are feeling as all the tension leaves. Start breathing deeply when you get to your chest muscles. By the time you have found your chair, you will be so relaxed it will feel like bliss!

Fight distraction

A lucky few are able to focus deeply when taking an important examination, but most people are easily distracted, probably because they would rather be any place else! There are several things you can do to protect yourself from distraction.

Stay away from windows. If you sit near a window you are adding an unnecessary distraction.

Choose a seat away from the aisle so you do not become distracted by people who leave early. People who leave the exam room early are often the ones who fail. Do not compare your time to theirs.

Of course, you love your friends; that's why they are your friends! In the test room, however, they should become complete strangers inside your mind. Forget they are there. The first step is to physically distance yourself from friends or classmates. That way, you will not be tempted to glance at them to see how they are doing, and there will be no chance of eye contact that could either distract you or even lead to an accusation of cheating. Furthermore, if they are feeling stressed because they did not spend the focused time studying that you did, their anxiety is less likely to permeate your hard-earned calm.

Of course, you will want to choose a seat where there is sufficient light. Nothing is worse than trying to take an important examination under flickering lights or dim bulbs.

Ask the instructor or exam proctor to close the door if there is a lot of noise outside. If the instructor or proctor is unable to do so, block out the noise as best you can. Do not let anything disturb you.

The TABE© does not allow any personal items in the exam room. A four-function calculator is permitted for the applied mathematics portion, and pencils and scrap paper are also provided. Eat protein, complex carbohydrates and a little fat to keep you feeling full and to supercharge your energy. Nothing is worse than a sudden drop in blood sugar during an exam.

Do not allow yourself to become distracted by being too cold or hot. Regardless of the weather outside, carry a sweater, scarf or jacket if the air conditioning at the test site is set too high, or the heat set too low. By the same token, dress in layers so that you are prepared for a range of temperatures.

Watch Caffeine

Drinking a gallon of coffee or gulping a few energy drinks might seem like a great idea, but it is, in fact, a very bad one. Caffeine, pep pills or other artificial sources of energy are more likely to leave you feeling rushed and ragged. Your brain might be clicking along, all right, but chances are good it is not clicking along on the right track! Furthermore, drinking coffee or energy drinks will mean frequent trips to the rest room. This will cut into the time you should be spending answering questions and is a distraction in itself, since each time you need to leave the room you lose focus. Pep pills will only make it harder for you to think straight when solving complicated problems.

At the same time, if anxiety is your problem try to find ways around using tranquilizers during test-taking time. Even medically prescribed anti-anxiety medication can make you less alert and even decrease your motivation. Being motivated is what you need to get you through an exam. If your anxiety is so bad that it threatens to interfere with your ability to take an exam, speak to your doctor and ask for documentation. Many testing sites will allow non-distracting test rooms, extended testing time and other accommodations with a doctor's note that explains the situation is made available.

Keep Breathing

It might not make a lot of sense, but when people become anxious, tense, or scared, their breathing becomes shallow and, sometimes stop breathing all together! Pay attention to your emotions, and when you are feeling worried, focus on your breathing. Take a moment to remind yourself to breathe deeply and regularly. Drawing in steady, deep breaths energizes the body. When you continue to breathe deeply you will notice you exhale all the tension.

If you feel you need to, try rehearsing breathing at home. With continued practice of this relaxation technique, you will begin to know the muscles that tense up under pressure. Call these your "signal muscles." These are the ones that will speak to you first, begging you to relax. Take the time to listen to those muscles and do as they ask. With just a little breathing practice, you will get into the habit of checking yourself regularly and when you realize you are tense, relaxation will become second nature.

Avoid Anxiety Before a Test

Manage your time effectively

This is a key to your success! You need blocks of uninterrupted time to study all the pertinent material. Creating and maintaining a schedule will help keep you on track, and will remind family members and friends that you are not available. Under no circumstances should you change your blocks of study time to accommodate someone else, or cancel a study session to do something more fun. Do not interfere with your study time for any reason!

Relax

Use whatever works best for you to relieve stress. Some folks like a good, calming stretch with yoga, others find expressing themselves through journaling to be useful. Some hit the floor for a series of crunches or planks, and still others take a slow stroll around the garden. Integrate a little relaxation time into your schedule, and treat that time, too, as sacred.

Eat healthy

Instead of reaching for the chips and chocolate, fresh fruits and vegetables are not only yummy but offer nutritional benefits that help to relieve stress. Some foods accelerate stress instead of reducing it and should be avoided. Foods that add to higher anxiety include artificial sweeteners, candy and other sugary foods, carbonated sodas, chips, chocolate, eggs, fried foods, junk foods, processed foods, red meat, and other foods containing preservatives or heavy spices. Instead, eat a bowl of berries and some yogurt!

Get plenty of ZZZZZZZs

Do not cram or try to do an all-nighter. If you created a study schedule at the beginning, and if you have stuck with that schedule, have confidence! Staying up too late trying to cram in last-minute bits of information is going to leave you exhausted the next day. Besides, whatever new information you cram in will only displace all the important ideas you've spent weeks learning. Remember: You need to be alert and fully functional the day of the exam

Have confidence in yourself!

Everyone experiences some anxiety when taking a test, but exhibiting a positive attitude banishes anxiety and fills you with the knowledge you really do know what you need to know. This is your opportunity to show how well prepared you are. Go for it!

Be sure to take everything you need

Depending on the exam, you may be allowed to have a pen or pencil, calculator, dictionary or scratch paper with you. Have these gathered together along with your entrance paperwork and identification so that you are sure you have everything that is needed.

Do not chitchat with friends

Let your friends know ahead of time that it is not anything personal, but you are going to ignore them in the test room! You need to find a seat away from doors and windows, one that has good lighting, and get comfortable. If other students are worried their anxiety could be detrimental to you; of course, you do not have to tell your friends that. If you are afraid they will be offended, tell them you are protecting them from your anxiety!

Common Test-Taking Mistakes

Taking a test is not much fun at best. When you take a test and make a stupid mistake that negatively affects your grade, it is natural to be very upset, especially when it is something that could have been easily avoided. So what are some of the common mistakes that are made on tests?

Do not fail to put your name on the test

How could you possibly forget to put your name on a test? You would be amazed at how often that happens. Very often, tests without names are thrown out immediately, resulting in a failing grade.

Marking the wrong multiple-choice answer

It is important to work at a steady pace, but that does not mean bolting through the questions. Be sure the answer you are marking is the one you mean to. If the bubble you need to fill in or the answer you need to circle is 'C', do not allow yourself to get distracted and select 'B' instead.

Answering a question twice

Some multiple-choice test questions have two very similar answers. If you are in too much of a hurry, you might select them both. Remember that only one answer is correct, so if you choose more than one, you have automatically failed that question.

Mishandling a difficult question

We recommend skipping difficult questions and returning to them later, but beware! First, be certain that you do return to the question. Circling the entire passage or placing a large question mark beside it will help you spot it when you are reviewing your test. Secondly, if you are not careful to skip the question, you can mess yourself up badly. Imagine that a question is too difficult and you decide to save it for later. You read the next question, which you know the answer to, and you fill in that answer. You continue to the end of the test then return to the difficult question only to discover you didn't actually skip it! Instead, you inserted the answer to the following question in the spot reserved for the harder one, thus throwing off the remainder of your test!

Incorrectly Transferring an answer from scratch paper

This can happen easily if you are trying to hurry! Double check any answer you have figured out on scratch paper, and make sure what you have written on the test itself is an exact match!

Thinking too much

Oftentimes, your first thought is your best thought. If you worry yourself into insecurity, your self-doubts can trick you into choosing an incorrect answer when your first impulse was the right one!

Conclusion

CONGRATULATIONS! You have made it this far because you have applied yourself diligently to practicing for the exam and no doubt improved your potential score considerably! Passing your up-coming exam is a huge step in a journey that might be challenging at times but will be many times more rewarding and fulfilling. That is why being prepared is so important.

Good Luck!

Register for Free Updates and More Practice Test Questions

Register your purchase at

https://www.test-preparation.ca/register/ for fast and convenient access to updates, errata, free test tips and more practice test questions.

https://www.facebook.com/CompleteTestPreparation/

https://www.youtube.com/user/MrTestPreparation

Taking a test? We can help!

Complete study guides, practice questions, tutorials, study tips and more:

www.test-preparation.ca

What Students Say!

Visit our Online Library of student tips and strategies

https://www.test-preparation.ca/test-prep-and-studying-what-students-say/

Online Resources

How to Prepare for a Test - The Ultimate Guide

https://www.test-preparation.ca/the-ultimate-guide-to-test-preparation-strategy/

Learning Styles - The Complete Guide

https://www.test-preparation.ca/learning-styles/

Test Anxiety Secrets!

https://www.test-preparation.ca/how-to-overcome-test-anxiety/

Time Management on a Test

https://www.test-preparation.ca/test-tactics-the-time-wise-approach/

Flash Cards - The Complete Guide

https://www.test-preparation.ca/test-preparation-with-flash-cards/

Test Preparation Video Series

https://www.test-preparation.ca/video-series-on-test-preparation-multiple-choice-strategies-and-how-to-study/

How to Memorize - The Complete Guide

https://www.test-preparation.ca/a-guide-to-memorizing-anything-easily-and-painlessly/

www.ingramcontent.com/pod-product-compliance
Lightning Source LLC
Chambersburg PA
CBHW071845080526
44589CB00012B/1112